CAMBRIDGE TEXTS IN THE
HISTORY OF PHILOSOPHY

———

IMMANUEL KANT
*Groundwork of the Metaphysics
of Morals*

CAMBRIDGE TEXTS IN THE HISTORY OF PHILOSOPHY

Series editors

KARL AMERIKS
Professor of Philosophy, University of Notre Dame

DESMOND M. CLARKE
Emeritus Professor of Philosophy, University College Cork

The main objective of Cambridge Texts in the History of Philosophy is to expand the range, variety, and quality of texts in the history of philosophy which are available in English. The series includes texts by familiar names (such as Descartes and Kant) and also by less well-known authors. Wherever possible, texts are published in complete and unabridged form, and translations are specially commissioned for the series. Each volume contains a critical introduction together with a guide to further reading and any necessary glossaries and textual apparatus. The volumes are designed for student use at undergraduate and postgraduate level, and will be of interest not only to students of philosophy but also to a wider audience of readers in the history of science, the history of theology, and the history of ideas.

For a list of titles published in the series, please see end of book.

IMMANUEL KANT

———

Groundwork of the Metaphysics of Morals

TRANSLATED AND EDITED BY

MARY GREGOR

AND

JENS TIMMERMANN

University of St. Andrews

TRANSLATION REVISED BY

JENS TIMMERMANN

WITH AN INTRODUCTION BY

CHRISTINE M. KORSGAARD

Harvard University

Revised Edition

CAMBRIDGE
UNIVERSITY PRESS

CAMBRIDGE UNIVERSITY PRESS
Cambridge, New York, Melbourne, Madrid, Cape Town,
Singapore, São Paulo, Delhi, Mexico City

Cambridge University Press
The Edinburgh Building, Cambridge CB2 8RU, UK

Published in the United States of America by Cambridge University Press, New York

www.cambridge.org
Information on this title: www.cambridge.org/9781107008519

First published 1998 and reprinted eighteen times
Revised edition first published 2012

Printed in the United Kingdom at the University Press, Cambridge

A catalogue record for this publication is available from the British Library

ISBN 978-1-107-00851-9 Hardback
ISBN 978-1-107-40106-8 Paperback

Contents

Preface to the revised edition

The translation of this new edition of Immanuel Kant's *Groundwork of the Metaphysics of Morals* first appeared in my German–English edition (Cambridge, 2011). It is based on Mary Gregor's English version, first published by Cambridge University Press in 1996 and subsequently reprinted in the Cambridge Texts in the History of Philosophy.

Throughout the revision process, care was taken to preserve the familiar feel of Gregor's work. While there were many changes in matters of detail, explained in the introduction and notes to the bilingual edition, the principles of her approach – combining a high degree of faithfulness to Kant's German with readability and fluency – naturally remained intact.

The *Groundwork* was first published in 1785. The translation follows the German text of the German–English volume, which is based on the second original edition of 1786. All major departures of the second original edition from the first are documented in the footnotes of this volume.

For this new edition within the Cambridge Texts in the History of Philosophy, Professor Korsgaard has kindly brought her introduction and her note on further reading up to date to take account of recent developments in Kantian ethics. The notes and the selected glossary have been rewritten. I should like to thank Keith Bustos (St. Andrews) for his work on the revised index.

J.T.

Introduction

CHRISTINE M. KORSGAARD

A life devoted to the pursuit of philosophical inquiry may be inwardly as full of drama and event – of obstacle and overcoming, battle and victory, challenge and conquest – as that of any general, politician, or explorer, and yet be outwardly so quiet and routine as to defy biographical narration. Immanuel Kant was born in 1724 in Königsberg, East Prussia, to a Pietist family of modest means.[1] Encouraged by his mother and the family pastor to pursue the career marked out by his intellectual gifts, Kant attended the University of Königsberg, and then worked for a time as a private tutor in the homes of various families in the neighborhood, while pursuing his researches in natural science. Later he got a position as a *Privatdozent*, an unsalaried lecturer who is paid by student fees, at the University. There Kant lectured on logic, metaphysics, ethics, geography, anthropology, mathematics, the foundations of natural science, and physics. In 1770, he finally obtained a regular professorship, the Chair of Logic and Metaphysics, at Königsberg. Destined by limited means and uneven health never to marry or travel, Kant remained in the Königsberg area, a quiet, hardworking scholar and teacher, until his death in 1804.

But sometime in the 1770s – we do not know exactly when – Kant began to work out ideas that were destined to challenge our conception of reason's relationship – and so of our own relationship – to the world around us. Kant himself compared his system to that of Copernicus, which explained the ordering of the heavens by turning them inside out, that is, by removing the earth – the human world – from the center, and making it revolve around the sun instead. Kant's own revolution also turns the world inside out, but in a very different way, for it places humanity back in the center. Kant argued that the rational order which the metaphysician looks for in the world is neither something that we discover through experience, nor something that our reason assures us must be there. Instead, it is something which we human beings impose upon the world – in part through the way we construct our knowledge, but also, in a different way, through our actions.

The implications for moral philosophy, first presented in the *Groundwork of the Metaphysics of Morals*, are profound. The *Groundwork* is an acknowledged philosophical classic, an introduction to one of the most influential accounts of our moral nature which the tradition has ever produced. Some of its central themes – that every human being is an end in himself or herself, not to be used as a mere means by others; that respect for your own humanity finds its fullest expression in respect for that of others; and that morality is freedom, and evil a form of enslavement – have become not only well-established themes in moral philosophy, but part of our moral culture.

But the *Groundwork* owes its popularity to its power, not to its accessibility. Like all of Kant's works, it is a difficult book. It is couched in the technical vocabulary which Kant developed for the presentation of his ideas. It presents us with a single, continuous argument, each of whose steps is itself an argument, and which runs the length of the book. But the particular arguments which make up the whole are sufficiently difficult in themselves that their contribution to the larger argument is easy to lose sight of. The main aim of this introduction will be to provide a kind of road map through the book, by showing how the material presented in each of the main sections contributes to the argument as a whole. First, however, we must situate the project of the *Groundwork* within Kant's general project, and explain some of the basic terminology he employs.

Kant's philosophical project

Kant was led to his revolutionary views about reason through an investigation of the question "What contribution does pure reason make to our knowledge of the world and to the government of our actions?" The empiricists of Kant's day had claimed that all of our knowledge, as well as our moral ideas, is derived from experience. The more extreme of the rationalists, on the other hand, believed that at least in principle all truths could be derived from self-evident rational principles. And all rationalists believe that at least some important truths, such as the existence of God, the immortality of the soul, and truths about what we ought to do, are either self-evident or can be deductively proved. In order to formulate the issue between these two schools of thought more clearly, Kant employed two distinctions that apply to judgments. Since Kant uses these two distinctions in the *Groundwork* in order to formulate the question he wants to raise about morality, it is necessary for the reader to be acquainted with them.

The first is the analytic/synthetic distinction, which concerns what makes a judgment true or false. A judgment is analytic if the predicate is contained in the concept of the subject. Otherwise, the predicate adds something new to our conception of the subject and the judgment is synthetic. Analytic judgments are, roughly, true by definition: when we say that a moon is a satellite of a planet, we are not reporting the results of an astronomical discovery, but explaining the meaning of a term. The second is the a priori/a posteriori distinction, which concerns the way we know that a judgment is true. A judgment is known a posteriori if it is known from experience, while it is known a priori if our knowledge of it is independent of any particular experience. Putting these two distinctions together yields three possible types of judgment. If a judgment is analytically true, we know this a priori, for we do not need experience to tell us what is contained in our concepts. For this reason, there are no analytic a posteriori judgments. If a judgment is known a posteriori, or from experience, it must be synthetic, for the subject and the predicate are "synthesized" in our experience: we learn from experience that the sky is blue, rather than yellow, because we see that the sky and blueness are joined. The remaining kind of judgment, synthetic a priori, would be one which tells us something new about its subject, and yet which is known independently of experience – on the basis of reasoning alone. If pure reason tells us anything substantial and important, either about the world, or about what we ought to do, then what it tells us will take the form of synthetic a priori judgments. So for Kant, the question whether pure reason can guide us, either in metaphysical speculation or in action, amounts to the question whether and how we can establish any synthetic a priori judgments.[2]

The Preface, and the project of the *Groundwork*

We can make these abstract ideas more concrete by turning to the Preface of the *Groundwork*. Here Kant divides philosophy into three parts: *logic*, which applies to all thought; *physics*, which deals with the way the world is; and *ethics*, which deals with what we ought to do. Kant thinks of each of these as a domain of laws: logic deals with the laws of thought; physics, with the laws of nature; and ethics, with what Kant calls the laws of freedom, that is, the laws governing the conduct of free beings. Logic is a domain of pure reason, but physics and ethics each have both a pure and an empirical part. For instance, we learn about particular laws of nature, such as the law that viruses are the cause of colds, from experience. But how do we learn that the world in general behaves in a lawlike way – that every event has a cause?[3] This judgment is not based on experience, for we can have no experience of every possible event. Nor is it an analytic judgment, for it is not part of the concept of an event that it has a cause. If we do know, then, that the world in general behaves in a lawlike way, we must have synthetic a priori knowledge. A body of such knowledge is called a "metaphysics." If it is true that every event has a cause, then this truth is part of the metaphysics of nature.

That there must be a metaphysics of morals is even more obvious. For morality is concerned with practical questions – not with the way things *are*, but with the way things *ought to be*. Since experience tells us only about the way things are, it cannot by itself provide answers to our practical questions. Moral judgments must therefore be a priori. Yet it is clear that moral laws are not analytic, for if they were, we could settle controversial moral questions simply by analyzing our concepts. So if there are any moral requirements, then there must be a metaphysics of morals, a body of synthetic a priori judgments concerning what we ought to do.

The *Groundwork*, however, is not Kant's entire metaphysics of morals, but only its most fundamental part. Kant wrote another book under the title *The Metaphysics of Morals*, in which our duties are categorized and expounded in considerable detail. There the reader may learn what conclusions Kant himself thought could be derived from his theory about a wide variety of issues, ranging from questions of personal morality – such as the legitimacy of suicide, the permissibility of using alcohol and drugs, the proper treatment of animals, and the nature and conduct of friendship and marriage – to larger political questions, such as the proper form of the political state, the legitimacy of revolution, and the permissibility of war.

This book is only a *Groundwork*, and its aim is to establish the most preliminary and fundamental point of the subject: that there is a domain of laws applying to our conduct, that there is such a thing as morality. Its aim is, as Kant himself says, "the identification and corroboration *of the supreme principle of morality*" (4:392).[4] That supreme principle, which Kant calls the *categorical imperative*, commands simply that our actions should have the *form* of moral conduct; that is, that they should be derivable from universal principles. When we act, we are to ask whether the reasons for which we propose to act could be made universal, embodied in a principle. Kant believed that this formal requirement yields substantive constraints on our conduct – not every proposed reason for action can be made universal, and so not every action can be squared with the requirement of acting on principle. We have already seen that the principle that tells us that nature in general behaves in a lawlike way must be synthetic a priori, if it can be established at all. In the same way, Kant thinks, the principle that tells us that *we ought to* behave in a lawlike way must be synthetic a priori, if ethics exists at all. The project of the *Groundwork* is simply to establish that there is a categorical imperative – and so that we have moral obligations.

First section

In each section of the *Groundwork*, Kant carries out a specific project, which in turn forms part of the argument of the whole. In the Preface, Kant says that his project in the first section will be "to take one's route analytically from common cognition to the determination of its supreme principle" (4:392). In other words, Kant is going to start from our ordinary ways of thinking about morality and analyze them to discover the principle behind them. It is important to keep in mind that because he is analyzing our ordinary views, Kant is not, in this section, trying to *prove* that human beings have obligations. Instead, he is trying to identify *what* it is that he has to establish in order to prove that. What must we show, in order to show that moral obligation is real?

The "common cognition" from which Kant starts his argument is that morally good actions have a special kind of value. A person who does the right thing for the right reason evinces what Kant calls a good will, and the first section opens with the claim that a good will is the only thing to which we attribute "unconditional worth." The good will is good "just by its willing" (4:394), which means that it is in actions expressive of a good will that we see this special kind of value realized. Kant does not mean that the good will is the only thing we value for its own sake, or as an end. A number of the things which Kant says have only "conditional" value, such as health and happiness, are things obviously valued for their own sakes. Instead, he means that the good will is the only thing which has a value that is completely independent of its relation to other things, which it therefore has in all circumstances, and which cannot be undercut by external conditions.

A scientist may be brilliant at his work, and yet use his gifts for evil ends. A political leader may achieve fine ends, but be ruthless in the cost she is willing to impose on others in order to carry out her plans. A wealthy aesthete may lead a gracious and happy life, and yet be utterly regardless of the plight of less fortunate people around him. The evil ends of the scientist, the ruthlessness of the politician, and the thoughtlessness of the aesthete undercut or at least detract from what we value in them and their lives. But suppose that someone performs a morally worthy action: say, he hurries to the rescue of an endangered enemy, at considerable risk to himself. Many things may go wrong with his action. Perhaps the rescuer fails in his efforts to save his enemy. Perhaps he himself dies in the attempt. Perhaps the attempt was ill judged; we see that it could not have worked and so was a wasted effort. In spite of all this, we cannot withhold our tribute from this action, and from the rescuer as its author. Nothing can detract from the value of such an action, which is independent of "what it effects, or accomplishes" (4:394).[5]

When we attribute unconditional value to an action, it is because we have a certain conception of the motives from which the person acted. If we found out, for instance, that the rescuer had acted only because he hoped he would get a reward, and had no idea that there was any risk involved, we would feel quite differently. So what gives a morally good action its special value is the motivation behind it, the principle on the basis of which it is chosen, or in Kantian terms, willed. This implies that once we know how actions with unconditional value are willed – once we know what principle a person like the rescuer acts on – we will know what makes them morally good. And when we know what makes actions morally good, we will be able to determine *which* actions are morally good, and so to determine what the moral law tells us to do. This is what Kant means when he says he is going to "unravel the concept" of a good will (4:397): that he is going to find out what principle the person of good will acts on, in order to determine what the moral law tells us to do.

In order to do this, Kant says, he is going to focus on a particular category of morally good actions, namely those which are done "from duty." Duty is the good will operating under "certain subjective limitations and hindrances, which ... far from concealing it and making it unrecognizable... bring it out by contrast and make it shine forth all the more brightly" (4:397). The hindrance Kant has in mind is that the person of whom we say that he acts "from duty" has other motives which, in the absence of duty, would lead him to avoid the action. When such a person does his duty, not otherwise wanting to, we know that the thought of duty alone has been sufficient to produce the action. Looking at this kind of case, where the motive of duty produces an action without any help from other motives, gives us a clearer view of what that motive is.[6]

Kant proceeds to distinguish three kinds of motivation. You may perform an action *from duty*, that is, do it because you think it is the right thing to do. You may perform it from *immediate inclination*, because you want to do it for its own sake, or because you enjoy doing actions of that kind. Or, finally, you may perform an action because you are "impelled to do so by another inclination," that is, as a means to some further end (4:397). In order to discover what is distinctive about good-willed actions and so what their principle is, Kant invites us to think about the contrast between right actions done from duty and right actions motivated in these other ways. To illustrate this contrast, he provides some examples.

The first one involves a merchant who refrains from overcharging gullible customers, because this gives him a good reputation which helps his business. This is an example of the third kind of motivation – doing what is right, but only as a means to some further end – and Kant mentions it only to lay it aside. The difference between doing the right thing from duty and doing it to promote some other end is obvious, for someone who does the right thing from duty does it for its own sake, and not for any ulterior motive. Yet in order that an action should evince a good will, it is not enough that it should be done for its own sake. This is the point of the other three examples, in which Kant contrasts someone who does an action from immediate inclination with someone who does the same action from duty. For instance, Kant says, there are people

> so attuned to compassion that, even without another motivating ground of vanity, or self-interest, they find an inner gratification in spreading joy around them, and can relish the contentment of others, in so far as it is their work. (4:398)

A person like this helps others when they are in need, and, unlike the prudent merchant, but *like* the dutiful person, does so for its own sake. A sympathetic person has no ulterior purpose in helping; he just enjoys "spreading joy around him." The lesson Kant wants us to draw from this is that the difference between the sympathetic person, and the person who helps from the motive of duty, does not rest in their purposes. They have the same purpose, which is to help others. Yet the sympathetic person's action does not have the moral worth of the action done from duty. According to Kant, reflection on this fact leads us to see that the moral worth of an action does not lie in its purpose, but rather in the "maxim" on which it is done, that is, the principle on which the agent acts (4:399).

In order to understand these claims it is necessary to understand the psychology behind them: the way that, as Kant sees it, human beings decide to act. According to Kant, our nature presents us with "incentives" which prompt or tempt us to act in certain ways. Among these incentives are the psychological roots of our ordinary desires and inclinations (as sympathy is the root of the desire to help); later, we will learn that moral thoughts – thoughts about what is required of us – also provide us with incentives. These incentives do not operate on us directly as causes of decision and action. Instead, they provide considerations which we take into account when we decide what to do. When you decide to act on an incentive, you "make it your maxim" to act in the way suggested by the incentive. For instance, when you decide to do something simply because you want to, you "make it your maxim" to act as desire prompts.

Kant claims that the difference between the naturally sympathetic person and the dutiful person rests in their maxims. The sympathetic person decides to help because helping is something he enjoys. His maxim, therefore, is to do those things he likes doing. The point here is not that his *purpose* is simply to please himself. His purpose is to help, but he adopts that purpose – he makes it his maxim to pursue that end – because he enjoys helping. The reason his action lacks moral worth is not that he *wants* to help only because it *pleases* him. The reason his action lacks moral worth is that he *chooses* to help *only* because he *wants* to: he allows himself to be guided by his desires in the selection of his ends. The person who acts from duty, by contrast, makes it her maxim to help because she conceives helping as something that is required of her. Again we must understand this in the right way. The point is not that her *purpose* is "to do her duty." Her purpose is to help, but she chooses helping as her purpose *because* she thinks that is what she is required to do: she thinks that the needs of others make a claim on her.

Kant thinks that performing an action because you regard the action or its end as one that is required of you is equivalent to being moved by the thought of the maxim of the action as a kind of law. The dutiful person takes the maxim of helping others to *express* or *embody* a requirement, just as a law does. In Kant's terminology, she sees the maxim of helping others as having *the form of a law*.[7] When we think that a certain maxim expresses a requirement, or has the form of a law, that thought itself is an incentive to perform the action. Kant calls this incentive "respect for law."

We now know what gives actions done from duty their special moral worth. They get their moral worth from the fact that the person who does them acts from respect for law. A good person is moved by the thought that his or her maxim has the form of a law. The principle of a good will, therefore, is to do only those actions whose maxims can be conceived as having the form of a law. If there is such a thing as moral obligation – if, as Kant himself says, "duty is not to be as such an empty delusion and a chimerical concept" (4:402) – then we must establish that our wills are governed by this principle: "I ought never to act except in such a way that I could also will that my maxim should become a universal law."

Second section

Although the argument of the first section proceeded from our ordinary ideas about morality, and involved the consideration of examples, it is not therefore an empirical argument. The examples do not serve as a kind of data from which conclusions about moral motivation are inductively drawn. Instead, the argument is based on our rational appraisal of the people in the examples, taking the facts about their motivation as given: if these people act from respect for law, as the examples stipulate, then their actions have moral worth. Whether anyone has ever actually acted from respect for law is a question about which moral philosophy must remain silent. So demonstrating that the categorical imperative governs our wills is not a matter of showing that we actually act on it. Instead, it is a matter of showing that we act on it in so far as we are rational. A comparison will help here. Showing that the principle of non-contradiction governs our beliefs is not a matter of showing that no one ever in fact holds contradictory beliefs, for people surely do. Nor is it a matter of showing that people are sometimes moved, say, to give up cherished beliefs when they realize those beliefs will embroil them in contradiction. Instead, it is a matter of showing that in so far as they are rational, that's what they do. Kant's project in the second section therefore is to:

> trace and distinctly present the practical rational faculty from its general rules of determination up to where there arises from it the concept of duty. (4:412)

In other words, in the second section Kant lays out a theory of practical reason, in which the moral law appears as one of the principles of practical reason.

It is a law of nature, very roughly speaking, that what goes up must come down. Toss this book into the air, and it will obey that law. But it will not, when it reaches its highest point, say to itself, "I ought to go back down now, for gravity requires it." As rational beings, however, we do in this way reflect on, and sometimes even announce to ourselves, the principles on which we act. In Kant's words, we act not merely in accordance with laws, but in accordance with our representations or conceptions of laws (4:412).

Yet we human beings are not perfectly rational, since our desires, fears, and weaknesses may tempt us to act in irrational ways. This opens up the possibility of a gap between the principles upon which we actually act – our maxims or subjective principles – and the objective laws of practical reason. For this reason, we conceive the objective laws of practical reason as imperatives, telling us what we *ought* to do. The theory of practical reason is therefore a theory of imperatives.

Imperatives may be either hypothetical or categorical. A hypothetical imperative tells you that if you will something, you ought also to will something else: for example, if you will to be healthy, then you ought to exercise. That is an imperative of skill, telling you how to achieve some particular end. Kant believes that there are also hypothetical imperatives of prudence, suggesting what we must do given that we all will to be happy.

A categorical imperative, by contrast, simply tells us what we ought to do, not on condition that we will something else, but unconditionally.

Kant asks how all these imperatives are "possible" (4:417), that is, how we can establish that they are legitimate requirements of reason, binding on the rational will. He thinks that in the case of hypothetical imperatives the answer is easy. A hypothetical imperative is based on the principle that whoever wills an end, in so far as he is rational, also wills the means to that end. This principle is analytic, since *willing* an end, as opposed to merely wanting it or wishing for it or thinking it would be nice if it were so, is setting yourself to bring it about, to cause it. And setting yourself to cause something just is setting yourself to use the means to it. Since willing the means is conceptually contained in willing the end, if you will an end and yet fail to will the means to that end, you are guilty of a kind of practical contradiction.

Since a categorical imperative is unconditional, however, there is no condition given, like the prior willing of an end, which we can simply analyze to derive the "ought" statement. The categorical imperative must therefore be *synthetic*, so morality depends on the possibility of establishing a *synthetic a priori* practical principle.

The Formula of Universal Law

Kant does not, however, move immediately to that task; in fact, he will not be in a position to take that up until the third section. The second section, like the first, proceeds "analytically." Kant is still working towards uncovering *what* we have to prove *in order to* establish that moral requirements really bind our wills. The first step is to analyze the very idea of a categorical imperative in order to see what it "contains." Kant says:

> when I think of a categorical imperative I know at once what it contains. For since besides the law the imperative contains only the necessity of the maxim to conform with this law, whereas the law contains no condition to which it was limited, nothing is left but the universality of a law as such, with which the maxim of the action ought to conform, and it is this conformity alone that the imperative actually represents as necessary. (4:420–421)

This is the sort of thing that makes even practiced readers of Kant gnash their teeth. A rough translation might go like this: the categorical imperative is a law, to which our maxims must conform. But the reason they must do so cannot be that there is some *further* condition they must meet, or some *other* law to which they must conform. For instance, suppose someone proposed that we must keep our promises because it is the will of God that we should do so – the law would then "contain the condition" that our maxims should conform to the will of God. This would yield only a conditional requirement to keep our promises – "if you would obey the will of God, then you must keep your promises" – whereas the categorical imperative must give us an *unconditional* requirement. Since if the imperative is to be categorical there can be no such condition, all that remains is that the categorical imperative should tell us that our maxims themselves must be laws – that is, that they must be universal, that being the characteristic of laws.

There is a simpler way to make this point. What could make it true that we must keep our promises because it is the will of God? That would be true only if it were true that we must indeed obey the will of God, that is, if "obey the will of God" were itself a *categorical* imperative. Conditional requirements give rise to a regress; if there are unconditional requirements, we must at some point arrive at principles on which we are required to act, not because we are commanded to do so by some yet higher law, but because they are laws in themselves. The categorical imperative, in the most general sense, tells us to act on *those* principles, principles which are laws in themselves. Kant continues:

> There is, therefore, only a single categorical imperative and it is this:
> *act only according to that maxim through which you can at the same time will that it become a universal law.* (4:421)

Kant next shows us how this principle serves to identify our duties, by showing us that there are maxims which it rules out – maxims which we could not possibly will to become universal laws. He suggests that the way to test whether you can will your maxim as a universal law is by performing a kind of thought experiment, namely, asking whether you could will your maxim to be a law of nature in a world of which you yourself were going to be a part. He illustrates this with four examples, the clearest of which is the second.

A person in financial difficulties is considering "borrowing" money on the strength of a false promise. He needs money, and knows he will get it only if he says to another person, "I promise you I will pay you back next week." He also knows perfectly well that he will not be able to repay the money when next week comes. His question is whether he can will that the maxim of making a false promise in order to get some money should become a law of nature. Although Kant does not do this, it helps to set out the test in a series of steps.

The first step is to formulate the maxim. In most cases, the person is considering doing a certain act for a certain end, so the basic form of the maxim is "I will do Act-A in order to achieve Purpose-P." Suppose then that your maxim is:

> I will make a false promise in order to get some ready cash.

Next we formulate the corresponding "law of nature." It would be:

> Everyone who needs some ready cash makes a false promise.

At least where duties to others are concerned, Kant's test may be regarded as a formalization of the familiar moral challenge: "What if everybody did that?" In order to answer this question, you are to imagine a world where everybody does indeed do that. We might call this the "World of the Universalized Maxim." At this point it is important to notice that Kant says the categorical imperative tells you to act on a maxim which you can *at the same time* will to be a universal law: he means at the same time as you will the maxim itself. So you are to imagine that you are in the World of the Universalized Maxim, seeing whether you can will to act on your maxim in that world. For instance, you imagine that you are asking whether you could will to secure some ready cash by means of a false promise in a world where everyone who needs a little ready cash (tries to) secure it by means of a false promise. In particular, you are asking whether any contradiction arises when you try to do that. Kant, says, in the example at hand, that it does, because:

> the universality of a law that everyone, once he believes himself to be in need, could promise whatever he fancies with the intention not to keep it, would make the promise and the end one may pursue with it itself impossible, as no one would believe he was being promised anything but would laugh about any such utterance, as a vain pretense. (4:422)

Why is this a contradiction? This question has attracted an enormous amount of philosophical attention and many interpretations have been proposed. The views that have been suggested may be divided into three broad categories.

Proponents of a logical contradiction interpretation think Kant means there is a straightforward logical contraction in the proposed law of nature. One might argue, for instance, that the universalization of the maxim of false promising would undercut the very practice of making and accepting promises, thus making promises impossible and the maxim literally inconceivable.[8]

Kant's use of teleological language in some of the examples has suggested to proponents of the teleological contradiction interpretation that the contradiction emerges only when the maxim is conceived as a possible teleological law of nature. False promising violates the "natural purpose" of promising, which is to create trust and cooperation, so that a universal law of false promising could not serve as part of a teleological system of natural laws.

According to proponents of the practical contradiction interpretation, the maxim's efficacy in achieving its purpose would be undercut by its universalization. In willing its universalization, therefore, the agent would be guilty of the same sort of practical contradiction that is involved in the violation of a hypothetical imperative. In fact, the maxim in the example is derived from a hypothetical imperative – "if you need some ready cash, you ought to make a false promise" – which in turn is derived from a "law of nature" or "causal law" – namely that false promising is a cause of, and so a means to, the possession of ready cash. In the World of the Universalized Maxim, however, this law no longer obtains. So in willing the World of the Universalized Maxim the agent undercuts the causal law behind the hypothetical imperative from which his own maxim is derived, making his own method of getting the money ineffective. Language supporting all three of these interpretations can be found in Kant's texts, and different interpretations fit different examples better. The problem of finding a single account of the contradiction test that produces the right answers in all cases is one on which Kantians are still at work.

The question is complicated by the fact that Kant himself thinks contradictions may arise in two different ways (4:421, 4:424). In some cases, he says, the maxim cannot even be thought as a universal law of nature: the contradiction is in the very conception of the universalized maxim as a law. The example we have been considering is of that kind: there could not *be* a law that everyone who needs money should make false promises, so the maxim fails what is often called "the contradiction in conception test." Maxims which fail this test are in violation of strict or perfect duties, particular actions or omissions we owe to particular people, such as the duty to keep a promise, tell the truth, or respect someone's rights. But there are also maxims which we can conceive as universal laws, but which it would still be contradictory to *will* as laws: these maxims fail what is often called "the contradiction in the will test." They violate wide or imperfect duties, such as the duty to help others when they are in need, or to make worthwhile use of your talents.[9] Here again, there is disagreement about exactly what the contradiction is. Kant suggests that "all sorts of possible purposes" (4:423) would have to go unfulfilled in a world in which we had neglected our abilities and in which we could not count on the help of others when we are in need. Since rationality commits us to willing the means to our ends, we must will a world in which these most general means – our own abilities and the help of others – would be available to us.

These examples are offered simply as a few illustrations to show how the categorical imperative works to establish the moral status of our actions. Generally, if a maxim passes the categorical imperative test, the action is permissible; if it fails, the action is forbidden, and, in that case, the opposite action or omission is required. The maxims in the examples fail the test, showing, for instance, that making a false promise is forbidden, and that a commitment to helping others when they are in need is required. For a more complete account of what Kant thinks morality requires of us, however, the reader must look to the *Metaphysics of Morals*.

The thought experiment we have just considered shows us *how* to determine whether a maxim can be willed as a universal law, not *why* we should will only maxims that can be universal laws. Kant is not claiming that it is irrational to perform immoral actions because it actually embroils us in contradictions. The contradictions emerge only when we attempt to universalize our maxims, and the question why we must will our maxims as if they were to become universal laws remains to be answered. It is to this question Kant turns next.

The Formula of Humanity

We have now seen what the categorical imperative says. In order to show that we actually have unconditional requirements, and so that moral obligation is real, we have to show that this principle is one that necessarily governs our wills. This investigation is in part a motivational one, since no law can truly govern our wills unless we can be motivated by our awareness of its authority. Although Kant denies that we can ever know for certain that someone has been morally motivated, the moral law cannot have authority over our wills unless it is *possible* for us to be motivated by it. But Kant warns us that we cannot appeal to any empirical and contingent sources of motivation when making this argument. As we saw earlier, the sense in which we are trying to show that the moral law governs our wills is not that it actually moves us, either always or sometimes, but that it moves us in so far as we are rational. So the argument must show that the moral law has an authority capable of moving any rational being, and this means it must appeal only to the principles of pure rational psychology.

As rational beings, as Kant said before, we act in accordance with our representations or conceptions of laws. But what inspires us to formulate a maxim or a law ("what serves the will as the objective ground of its self-determination") is an end (4:427). Whenever we actually decide to take action, it is always with some end in view: either we regard the action as good in itself, or we are doing it as a means to some further end. If there are unconditional requirements, incumbent on all rational beings, then there must be ends that are necessarily shared by all rational beings – objective ends. Are there any such ends?

The ends that we set before ourselves in our ordinary actions, Kant urges, do not have absolute but only relative value: "merely their relation to a particular kind of desiderative faculty of the subject gives them their worth" (4:427). The point here is that most objects of human endeavor get the value that we assign them *from* the way in which they serve our needs, desires, and interests. Just as we value technology because it serves our needs, so we value pure science because we human beings, as Aristotle says, desire to know; we value the visual arts and music because of the way they arouse the human capacity for the disinterested enjoyment of sensory experience; we value literature and philosophy because they serve our thirst for self-understanding, and so forth. Although these other things are not mere means like technology, yet still the value that we assign them is not absolute or intrinsic, but relative to *our* nature. Yet, since we are rational beings, and we do pursue these things, we must think that they really are important, that there is reason to pursue them, that they are good. If their value does not rest in themselves, but rather in the fact that they are important to us, then in pursuing them, we are in effect taking ourselves to be important. In that sense, Kant says, it is a "subjective principle of human actions" that we treat *ourselves* as ends (4:429).

This suggests that the objective end which we need in order to explain why the moral law has authority for us is "the human being, and in general every rational being." Accordingly, the categorical imperative can now be reformulated as a law instructing us to respect the value of this objective end:

> *So act that you use humanity, in your own person as well as in the person of any other, always at the same time as an end, never merely as a means.* (4:429)

Using the same examples he used before, Kant proceeds to demonstrate how this principle can serve as a moral guide. Being of absolute value, human beings should not sacrifice themselves or one another for merely relatively valuable ends. Since it is in so far as we are rational beings that we accord ourselves this absolute value, the formula enjoins us to respect ourselves and each other *as* rational beings. So Kant thinks we should develop our own rational capacities, and promote one another's rationally chosen ends. Respecting someone as a rational being also means respecting her right to make her own decisions about her own life and actions. This leads to particularly strong injunctions against coercion and deception, since these involve attempts to take other people's decisions out of their own hands, to manipulate their wills for one's own ends. Someone who makes you a false promise in order to get some money, for instance, wants you to decide to give him the money. He predicts that you will not decide to give him the money unless he says he will pay it back, and therefore he says that he will pay it back, even though he cannot do so. His decision about what to say to you is entirely determined by what he thinks will *work* to get the result he wants. In that sense he treats your reason, your capacity for making decisions, as if it were merely an instrument for his own use. This is a violation of the respect he owes to you and your humanity.

This example brings out something important about Kant's conception of morality. What is wrong with the false promiser is not merely that he does not tell the truth. What is wrong with him is the *reason* that he does not tell the truth – because he thinks it will not get the result he wants –

and the attitude towards you which that reason embodies. Even if he told you the truth, if it were *only* because he thought it would get the result he wanted, he would *still* be regarding you as a mere means. Instead, we must tell others the truth so that they may exercise their own reason freely. And that means, that in telling them the truth, we are inviting them to reason together with us, to share in our deliberations. When we need the cooperation of others, we must be prepared to give them a voice in the decision about what it is to be done. These ideas lead Kant to a vision of an ideal human community, in which people reason together about what to do. Because this is the community of people who regard themselves and one another as ends in themselves, Kant calls it the kingdom of ends.

Autonomy and the kingdom of ends

To be rational is, *formally* speaking, to act on your representation of a law, whatever that law might be; but we have now seen that the content or *material* of the maxims or laws on which we act is given by the value we necessarily set upon our own humanity or rational nature. Putting these two ideas together leads us to a third idea, which is that as rational beings we make the law, we legislate it, for ourselves and each other. Suppose, for instance, I undertake a program of scientific research. I am curious, and wish to know; in treating my curiosity as a reason to undertake the research, I am in effect taking it to be good that I should know. Furthermore, since we have a duty to pursue one another's ends, my decision to pursue scientific research involves a claim on others: that they should recognize the value of my pursuit of this end, should not hinder it, and perhaps, under certain conditions, even offer help with it when I am in need. Thus my choice is an act of legislation: I lay it down, for myself and all others, that this research is a good thing, and shall be pursued. We may say that I *confer a value* upon scientific research, when I choose to pursue it. At the same time, however, the very fact that I make this claim on others whose humanity must be respected serves as a "*limiting condition*" on my own choice (4:431). If the end that I choose, or the means by which I choose to pursue it, is inconsistent with the value of humanity, then I cannot legislate it, and my choice is null and void: my maxim is not a law. Pulling these ideas together leads to what Kant describes as "the *principle* of every human will as *a will universally legislating through all its maxims*" (4:432).

This principle, Kant tells us, "would be very *well fitted* to be the categorical imperative" (4:432), because it suggests that the reason we are bound to obey the laws of morality is that we legislate these laws ourselves, that they are our own laws. According to Kant there are two ways in which we may be bound to conform to a law. Sometimes, we conform to a law because of some interest we have that is served by such conformity – for instance, when the law is supported by a sanction. If disobedience to the law will lead to our being fined, socially ostracized, thrown into prison, or dispatched to hell; or if obedience means we will be loved, saved, rewarded, or well-pleasing to God, we may consider ourselves bound to obey it for those reasons. At other times, however, we regard ourselves as bound to obey a law because we endorse the law itself, considered as a law: we think that this is indeed how people in general ought to act, and so we act that way ourselves. Kant calls the first sort of motivation heteronomous, because we are bound to the law by something outside of ourselves – God, the state, or nature – that attaches the sanction to the law. The second kind of motivation is autonomous, because we bind *ourselves* to the law. The principle that we give universal law through our maxims suggests that moral motivation is autonomous.[10]

And on reflection it seems that moral motivation must be autonomous. For if we are motivated to obey a law heteronomously, by a sanction, then the imperative we follow in obeying that law is a hypothetical imperative: *if* you would stay out of prison, or go to heaven, or whatever, *then* you must obey this law. And in that case, of course, the requirement is not unconditional after all. If categorical imperatives exist, then, it must also be true that human beings are capable of autonomous motivation. There can be only one reason why we must do what duty demands, and that is that we demand it of ourselves.

Earlier we saw that according to Kant's Copernican Revolution, the laws of reason are not something we find in the world, but rather something we human beings impose upon the world. We have now come around to the practical expression of that idea. Kant's predecessors, he believes, failed to discover the principle of morality, because they looked outside of the human will for the source of obligation, whereas obligation arises from, and so can only be traced to, the human capacity for self-government. Morality, on Kant's conception, is a kind of metaphysics in practice. We ourselves impose the laws of reason on our actions, and through our actions, on the world, when we act morally.

The principle of autonomy provides us with a third way of formulating the moral law: we should so act that we may think of ourselves as legislating universal laws through our maxims.[11] When we follow this principle we conceive ourselves as legislative citizens in the kingdom of ends. The kingdom of ends may be conceived either as a kind of democratic republic, "the systematic union of several rational beings through common laws" which the citizens make themselves; or as a system of all good ends, "a whole of all ends (of rational beings as ends in themselves, as well as the ends of its own that each of them may set for itself)" (4:433). The laws of the kingdom of ends are the laws of freedom, both because it is the mark of free citizens to make their own laws, and because the content of those laws directs us to respect each citizen's free use of his or her own reason. The conception of ourselves as legislative citizens is the source of the dignity we accord to human beings, a dignity which Kant, bringing the argument full circle, now equates with the unconditional value of a good will. We now know what gives the good will its unconditional value:

> It is nothing less than the *share* it obtains for a rational being *in universal legislation*, by which it makes it fit to be a member of a possible kingdom of ends. (4:435)

But we also now know what we need to do in order to complete the argument. Recall that morality is real if the moral law has authority for our wills. The argument of the second section has yet not shown this, but it has prepared the way, for we now know what has to be true of us if the moral law is to have authority for our wills. We must be autonomous beings, capable of being motivated by the conception of ourselves as legislative citizens in the kingdom of ends, citizens who are bound only by the laws that we give to ourselves. If Kant can show that we are autonomous, he will have shown that we are obligated by the moral law. This is the project of the third section.

Third section

Up until now, the argument has proceeded "analytically" (4:392). By analyzing our ordinary conception of moral value, and our conception of rational action, we have arrived at an idea of what the moral law says – it says to act only on a maxim you can will as a universal law – and at an idea of the characteristic in virtue of which a person is governed by the moral law – autonomy of the will. To complete the argument, Kant has to show that we and all rational beings really have the kind of autonomous wills for which the moral law is authoritative. This is not an analytic claim, yet if it is to hold for all rational beings it must be an a priori one. When a proposition is synthetic a priori, Kant now tells us, its two terms must be "bound together by their connection with a third thing in which they are both to be found"; that is, it must be deduced (4:447).

Kant opens the third section by making one of the two connections that his argument requires. The will is the causality of a rational being, for our will determines our actions, and it is through our actions that we have effects in the world. If the will's actions – its choices and decisions – were in turn determined by the laws of nature, then it would not be a *free* will. Suppose that all your choices were determined by a psychological law of nature, say, "a person's will is always determined by the strength of his desires." Although you would always do what you most strongly desire, your will would not, according to Kant's definition, be free. A free person is one whose actions are not determined by any external force, not even by his own desires.

This is merely a negative conception of freedom. But Kant thinks it points us towards a more positive conception of freedom. The will is a cause, and the concept of causality includes the idea of acting according to laws: since we identify something as a cause by observing the regularity of its effects, the idea of a cause which functions randomly is a contradiction. To put it another way, the will is practical reason, and we cannot conceive a practical reason which chooses and acts for no reason. Since reasons are derived from principles, the will must have a principle. A free will must therefore have its own law or principle, which it gives to itself. It must be an autonomous will. But the moral law just is the law of an autonomous will. Kant concludes that "a free will and a will under moral laws are one and the same" (4:447).

Readers are often taken aback by the ease with which Kant draws this conclusion. In the previous section, Kant showed that the authority of morality must be grounded in our autonomy – that moral laws must be laws which we give to ourselves. So any being who is governed by the moral law must be autonomous. But this argument depends on a reciprocal claim that looks at first as if it were stronger – namely, that any autonomous being must be governed by the moral law. Why does Kant think he has shown this? To see why, consider what the categorical imperative, in particular the Formula of Universal Law, says. The Formula of Universal Law tells us to choose a maxim that we can will as a law. The *only* condition that it imposes on our choices is that they have the form of law. *Nothing determines any content for that law; all that it has to be is a law.* As we have just seen, Kant thinks that a will, as a cause, must operate according to a law. If the will is free, then *nothing determines any content for that law; all that it has to be is a law.* What this shows is that the moral law just is the principle of a free will: to have a free will and to operate in accordance with the Formula of Universal Law are, as Kant puts it, "one and the same."

Freedom and morality are therefore analytically connected. A free will is one governed by the moral law, so if we have free wills, we are governed by the moral law. But do we have free wills? Kant points out that in so far as we are rational, we necessarily act "under the idea of freedom" (4:448). When you act rationally, you take yourself to *choose* your actions, not to be impelled into them, and you think that you could have chosen otherwise. Even if you act on a desire, you do not take the desire to impel you into the action – you think, rather, that you *choose* to satisfy it, that you adopt a maxim of satisfying it. Rational choices are therefore undertaken under a kind of presupposition of freedom. And this being so, Kant proposes, we must, when we make such choices, see ourselves as being bound by the laws of freedom. Rationality requires that we act under the idea of freedom, and freedom is government by the moral law, so rationality requires that we regard ourselves as governed by the moral law. Kant's argument seems complete.

But Kant is not satisfied with the argument.[12] He complains that the argument does not explain the interest we take in the ideas of morality. He reminds us of a conclusion already established: if we are morally motivated, we cannot be moved by any interest outside of morality, for if we do our duty for the sake of something else, we are acting on a hypothetical, rather than a categorical, imperative. But now Kant points out that we must nevertheless *take an interest* in moral ideas if we are to act on them. This is clearest when morality demands that we do something contrary to our happiness. Here, on the one hand, is something you badly want to do, something on which your happiness depends; but you find, on reflection, that it would be wrong. If you are to be moved by this reflection to refrain from the action, the very thought that you cannot will your maxim as a universal law must be capable of motivating you to refrain from performing the action. You must assign a worth to autonomous action, and to yourself as capable of it, in comparison with which your happiness "should be taken for nothing" (4:450). The argument, Kant complains, has not shown how this is possible. It has shown how we arrive at the *consciousness* of the moral law, but it has not shown how in such a case we can be *motivated* by that consciousness. And unless we can be motivated this way, we are not after all free and autonomous.

Kant does not doubt that we do in fact sometimes take an interest in autonomous action and in ourselves as capable of it. But for all that the argument has shown so far, this may be only because of the importance we already assign to morality itself. If we can do no better than this, the argument will be circular: we will have derived moral obligation from a freedom of will which we have attributed to ourselves only because of the importance we in any case grant to morality.

Now at this point, although Kant does not say so, he begins to appeal to ideas he worked out in the *Critique of Pure Reason*, so a brief digression will be useful. In the *Critique of Pure Reason*, Kant distinguishes two different ways of thinking about the world that are available to us. We can think of the world as it is in itself, or as he calls it there the *noumenal* world, or we can think of the world as it appears to us, or as he calls it there the *phenomenal* world. These two conceptions arise from reflection on our cognitive relation to the world. The world is given to us through our senses, it *appears* to us, and to that extent we are passive in the face of it. We must therefore think of the world as generating, or containing something which generates, those appearances – something which is their source, and gives them to us. We can only *know* the world in so far as it is phenomenal, that is, in so far as it is given to the senses. But we can *think* of it as noumenal. This way of looking at things is important here for two reasons.

Part of the project of the *Critique of Pure Reason*, as we have already seen, is to provide an argument for the synthetic a priori principle that every event has a cause. The argument which Kant presents there has an important consequence for our task here: namely, that the law that every event has a cause can be established, but only for the phenomenal world, that is, only for the world in so far as it is knowable, and not for the world as it is in itself. Now the law that every event has a cause is at odds with the idea of freedom, for freedom is the idea of a first or uncaused causality, a cause that is not determined by any other cause. The upshot of Kant's limitation of the causal principle to the sensible or phenomenal world is this: freedom cannot be an object of knowledge; the knowable world is deterministic. But this does not mean that there is no freedom, for freedom might characterize things as they are in themselves. Indeed, in a sense we must think of things in themselves this way, for we conceive them as the first causes or ultimate sources of the appearances. This means that what Kant is seeking here cannot be evidence or knowledge that we really are free. In his philosophy, that is impossible. Instead he is asking whether we have grounds for regarding ourselves as free.

And – to return now to the *Groundwork* – Kant does think there are such grounds, provided precisely by this distinction between appearances and things in themselves. For this distinction provides a rational being with "two standpoints from which it can consider itself, and recognize laws for the use of its powers, and consequently for all its actions" (4:452). When we view ourselves as members of the sensible or phenomenal world, we regard everything about ourselves, including inner appearances such as our own thoughts and choices, as parts of the sensible world, and therefore as governed by its causal laws. But in so far as we are rational beings, we also regard ourselves as the *authors* of our own thoughts and choices. That is to say, we regard *ourselves* as the first causes or ultimate *sources* of these inner appearances. In so far as we do so, we necessarily think of ourselves as members of the noumenal world, or as Kant calls it here the world of understanding. And because we must think of ourselves as members of the world of understanding, we inevitably think of ourselves as free, and so as autonomous. With this independent reason for regarding ourselves as free, the suspicion of a circle is removed.

Kant is now ready to explain how a categorical imperative is possible – what makes it authoritative for the rational will. We must see ourselves as belonging to both the world of sense and the world of understanding. In so far as we are members of the world of sense, our choices and actions, like everything else, fall under the laws of nature. But in so far as we are members of the world of understanding, we are free. Now because "*the world of understanding contains the ground of the world of sense, and hence also of its laws*" (4:453), we must suppose that in our capacity as members of the world of understanding, we give laws to ourselves as members of the world of sense. And this is what gives us obligations. The conception of ourselves as members of the world of understanding is a conception of ourselves as self-governing, and so as autonomous or moral beings.

Kant ends with some reflections on the nature and limits of practical philosophy. The argument we have just considered requires that we view ourselves in two different ways. As members of the world of understanding, we are free, yet as members of the world of sense, our actions are determined. Furthermore, determinism is an object of knowledge, or at least a feature of the world in so far as it is known, while freedom is only an object of thought or understanding. The two views we take of ourselves may at first seem incompatible, and, if they are, the fact that determinism is a feature of the knowable world may seem to give it priority. But in fact the two standpoints are so far from being incompatible, that both are absolutely necessary. For we realize that *something* must furnish us with the appearances from which the sensible world is constructed, that there must be a world of things in themselves which provides us with the appearances. And we know that if we are ourselves *agents*, who are the sources of some of these appearances (our own actions), then we must be among these things in themselves.

This is why we affirm that our freedom is real; but this does not mean that we can explain how freedom, or, to put the same thing another way, pure practical reason, is possible. To explain something just is to subsume it under causal laws, so freedom by its very nature cannot be explained. Nor, for a parallel reason, can we explain the interest we take in moral ideas, if we must explain an interest in terms of some other interest that it promotes, or some pleasure that it causes. Yet we can now say more about what the object of moral interest is. For if we act as befits members of the world of understanding, we may claim to be citizens of the real kingdom of ends, the community of rational beings who, through their actions, try to impose a rational order on the natural world of sense. What interests us in morality is:

> the glorious ideal of a universal kingdom of *ends in themselves* (of rational beings) to which we can belong as members only if we carefully conduct ourselves according to maxims of freedom as if they were laws of nature. (4:462–463)

Notes

1. Pietism was a religious movement which emphasized inner religious experience, self-examination, and morally good works. Its emphasis on the importance of morality is often thought to have been a strong influence on Kant.
2. For Kant's own introductory discussion of these distinctions see the Introduction to the *Critique of Pure Reason* (trans. Paul Guyer and Allen Wood, the Cambridge Edition of the Works of Immanuel Kant, Cambridge

University Press, 1998). The relevant passages may be found at A6–11/B10–14, using the standard method of citing this work, according to the page numbers in the first (A) and second (B) editions. The analytic/synthetic distinction was challenged in the twentieth century, most famously by W. V. Quine in his "Two Dogmas of Empiricism" (in *From a Logical Point of View*, 2nd edition, Cambridge, MA: Harvard University Press, 1961). How damaging this attack is to Kant's project is a matter of philosophical debate.

3. The principle that every event has a cause has been challenged by modern physics; modern scientists believe that at the level of the most fundamental particles and events it does not hold. An obvious question is what impact this has on Kant's argument. Must he give up the idea that the causal principle is a synthetic a priori truth, or is it enough for his purposes that events at the macro-level must still be causally ordered if the world is to be knowable? For our purposes here, the causal principle may still be used as an example of a synthetic a priori truth.

4. The standard German edition of Kant's works is issued under the auspices of the Prussian Academy (1900–). The standard method of citing passages from Kant's works, except for the *Critique of Pure Reason* (see note 2), refers to the pagination of this edition, and the page numbers are given in the margins of most translations. The citation method used in this introduction also gives the volume number in which the work is found. The citation says that the passage quoted is on page 392 of volume 4 of the Academy edition. An English translation of most of Kant's works has been published by Cambridge University Press under the general editorship of Paul Guyer and Allen Wood.

5. At 4:395–397, Kant supports these ideas with an argument to the effect that in a teleologically organized system of nature, the natural purpose of the rational will would be to realize the good will, or moral worth. Kant argues that in a teleological system of nature, we can never say that an organ, faculty, or arrangement exists to serve some natural purpose unless it is the fittest and best adapted organ, faculty, or arrangement for that purpose. The rational will, Kant argues, is not especially well adapted to produce happiness or any end outside of itself. Its purpose must therefore be to realize its own value. This argument is offered as a supplement, and the main argument does not depend on it. Kant himself did not believe that a teleological conception of nature has the status of knowledge, although he did consider it an importantly useful way of looking at things. The reader is referred to the *Critique of the Power of Judgment* (trans. Paul Guyer and Eric Matthews, the Cambridge Edition of the Works of Immanuel Kant, Cambridge University Press, 2002) for Kant's views on teleology.

6. According to a common misreading of the text at this point and of the examples that follow, Kant believes that actions can have moral worth only if they are done reluctantly or without the support of inclination. This is not Kant's view. He focuses on cases in which the moral motive operates by itself because he wants to get a clear view of it, not because he thinks that the

presence of other possible motives somehow prevents an agent from acting on it.

7. Both here and later on in the discussion of the Formula of Universal Law, Kant makes it clear that he thinks the lawlike character of a maxim is a matter of its *form* rather than its *matter*. What does this mean? The distinction between form and matter is an inheritance of Aristotelian metaphysics, in which the matter of a thing is the materials or parts of which it is constructed, while the form is the arrangement of those parts that enables the object to serve its characteristic function. For instance if the function of a house is to serve as a shelter, we would say that the matter of the house is the walls and the roof, and the form is the way those parts are arranged so as to keep the weather out and the objects within protected. The parts of a maxim are usually the act which is done and the end for the sake of which it is done. We can show that the lawlike character of the maxim is a matter of the way the parts are arranged, the form, by considering a triple of maxims like this:

1. I will keep my weapon, because I want it for myself.
2. I will keep your weapon, because I want it for myself.
3. I will keep your weapon, because you have gone mad and may hurt someone.

Maxims 1 and 3 are maxims of good actions, while maxim 2 is of a bad action. Yet maxims 1 and 2 have the same purpose, and maxims 2 and 3 involve the same act. So the lawlike character of the maxim rests neither in the purpose, nor in the act, which are the parts or matter of the maxim. Instead it rests in the way those parts are combined – and so in the form of the maxim. In a good maxim, the parts are so combined that the maxim can serve as a law: everyone could act on it.

8. For the notion of a practice and the logical dependence of actions falling under the practice on the existence of the practice itself, see John Rawls, "Two Concepts of Rules," *Philosophical Review* 64 (January 1955): 3–32; reprinted in *John Rawls: Collected Papers*, Cambridge, MA: Harvard University Press, 1999.

9. In the *Groundwork*, Kant lines up the distinction between the contradiction in conception test and the contradiction in the will test with the traditional distinction between perfect and imperfect duties (described above) at 4:421, and with a less familiar distinction between strict or narrow duties and wide duties at 4:424. This parallel might be taken to suggest that these are just two sets of names for the same distinction, or at any rate that the two distinctions coincide. But in the later *Metaphysics of Morals* Kant describes a category of duties which are characterized as perfect duties and yet which, because they are duties of virtue and all of those are wide, must be wide duties (6:421ff.). Kant explains the distinction between narrow and wide obligation in the *Metaphysics of Morals* at 6:390–394. We have a duty of narrow obligation when we are required to perform a particular action, while we have a duty of

wide obligation when we are required to adopt a certain general maxim (e.g. to promote the happiness of others) but have leeway as to how to carry the duty out. This explanation leaves the difference between the two distinctions unclear, and Kant never directly addresses the question how the two distinctions are related. If Kant's considered view is that these two distinctions do not coincide, we are left uncertain whether the contradiction in conception test is best understood as a test for perfect duties, or as a test for strict duties. These rather intricate issues about the categorization of duties matter to the reader of the *Groundwork* because one of the duties Kant uses as an example here – the duty not to commit suicide in order to avoid misery – is one of those apparently identified in the later work as a perfect duty of wide obligation. This should make us cautious about this example.

10. There is a difficulty with Kant's argument here: we could not really consider ourselves bound to conform to a law for the sake of being loved, saved, rewarded, or well-pleasing to God unless we felt ourselves bound to promote those ends themselves. But if we regarded ourselves as bound to promote those ends, we would regard the law which commanded us to perform them as a *categorical* imperative, not merely a hypothetical one. If Kant is right that categorical imperatives can bind us only through our autonomy, his argument is stronger than he realized: the *only* way we can be bound by a law is if recognition of its intrinsic legal character – which as the argument has already established must be a matter of its form – induces us to impose that law upon ourselves.

11. Kant supposes that his three formulations are equivalent, not only in the sense that they direct us to perform the same actions, but in the sense that they are different ways of saying the same thing. All of them embody the view that a rational being must be governed only by his or her own reason. Yet the claim that they are equivalent has been challenged by commentators. Some have argued that the Formulae of Humanity and Autonomy or the Kingdom of Ends are stronger formulae, yielding a more well-defined set of duties, than the Formula of Universal Law. Others have argued that the Formula of the Kingdom of Ends imports an idea not present in the earlier formulae, namely that our duties are owed *to* others as well as to ourselves.

12. At this point, we arrive at the most difficult passages in the book. There is scholarly controversy over the questions why exactly Kant was dissatisfied, and whether he should have been. Interpretation is complicated by the fact that Kant himself continued to work on this part of the argument in later writings, especially in the *Critique of Practical Reason* (5:30–50), and the version of the argument he presents there seems, at least on the surface, to be different, although there is also controversy about whether it really is so. In any case, for a full understanding of Kant's views on this point, study of the *Critique of Practical Reason* is indispensable.

Chronology

1770	Appointed Professor of Logic and Metaphysics at the University of Königsberg; Inaugural Dissertation entitled *On the Form and Principles of the Sensible and the Intelligible World*
1781	*Critique of Pure Reason*, first (A) edition
1783	*Prolegomena to Any Future Metaphysics*
1783	*Review of Schultz's Attempt at the Introduction to a Doctrine of Morals for all Human Beings Regardless of Different Religions*
1784	*Idea for a Universal History with a Cosmopolitan Aim*
1784	*An Answer to the Question: What is Enlightenment?*
1785	*Review of Herder's Ideas on the Philosophy of the History of Humanity*
1785	*On the Wrongfulness of Unauthorized Publication of Books*
1785	*Groundwork of the Metaphysics of Morals*
1786	*Conjectural Beginning of Human History*
1786	*Metaphysical Foundations of Natural Science*
1786	*What is Orientation in Thinking?*
1787	*Critique of Pure Reason*, second (B) edition
1788	*Critique of Practical Reason*
1788	*On the Use of Teleological Principles in Philosophy*
1790	*Critique of the Power of Judgment*, first edition
1791	*On the Miscarriage of all Philosophical Trials in Theodicy*
1793	*On the Common Saying: That May be Correct in Theory, but it is of No Use in Practice*
1793	*Critique of the Power of Judgment*, second edition
1793	*Religion within the Boundaries of Mere Reason*
1794	Kant is censured by King Friedrich Wilhelm II for distorting and debasing Christianity in *Religion within the Boundaries of Mere Reason*
1794	*The End of All Things*
1795	*Toward Perpetual Peace*
1796	Kant's last lecture
1797	*The Metaphysics of Morals*
1797	*On a Supposed Right to Lie from Philanthropy*
1798	*Anthropology from a Pragmatic Point of View*

Further reading

The Groundwork of the Metaphysics of Morals is, as its title states, only the groundwork of a more complete ethical system, which the reader will find developed in Kant's other ethical works. In the *Groundwork*'s preface, Kant mentions his plan to issue a metaphysics of morals and seems to suggest that a complete critique of practical reason may not be necessary (4:391). But in the event he did first write the *Critique of Practical Reason* (1788; trans. and ed. Mary Gregory with an Introduction by Andrews Reath, Cambridge University Press, 1997), the first part of which covers much of the same territory as the *Groundwork*, but in a rather different way. The foundational argument, in particular, is presented very differently, and it is a matter of debate whether the argument really is different, and whether that was one of Kant's reasons for deciding to write the book. But the second *Critique* also explores the connections between Kant's ethical ideas and the ideas of the *Critique of Pure Reason*, and raises important questions about the differences between theoretical and practical reason.

The Metaphysics of Morals (1797; trans. and ed. Mary Gregor with an Introduction by Roger Sullivan, Cambridge University Press, 1996) consists of two parts. In the first part, the *Metaphysical First Principles of the Doctrine of Right*, Kant integrates ideas from his moral theory with elements drawn from the natural law and social contract traditions to produce his own theory of law and the political state. This part of Kant's thought has received its first comprehensive critical treatment in the English language in Arthur Ripstein's *Force and Freedom: Kant's Legal and Political Philosophy* (Cambridge, MA: Harvard University Press, 2009). Another important recent treatment is Sharon Byrd and Joachim

Hruschka's *Kant's Doctrine of Right: A Commentary* (Cambridge University Press, 2010). In the second part, the *Metaphysical First Principles of the Doctrine of Virtue*, Kant explicates his views on personal morality. Kant also discussed moral issues in his course lectures, some of which have been published. (These are based on students' notes. Some of them are available in *Lectures on Ethics*, trans. Louis Infield, Indianapolis: Hackett Publishing Co., 1963; others in *Lectures on Ethics*, trans. and ed. Peter Heath and J. B. Schneewind, the Cambridge Edition of the Works of Immanuel Kant, Cambridge University Press, 1997.) In the Introduction to the *Metaphysics of Morals*, Kant explains why moral theory falls into these two parts, and in both the general introduction and the introduction to the second part he discusses his theory of moral psychology. For a complete understanding of Kant's views on moral psychology, however, one must turn to an unexpected place – the first book of *Religion within the Boundaries of Mere Reason* (1793; trans. and ed. Allen W. Wood and George di Giovanni with an Introduction by Robert Merrihew Adams, Cambridge University Press, 1998) where Kant turned his attention to questions about the nature of choice and moral responsibility.

In Kant's view, moral philosophy naturally extends to religion and politics for two reasons. First, Kant believed that political and religious ideas that have had a long history or that recur in many different cultures are likely to have a basis in pure practical reason – that is, in morality. In all three *Critiques*, Kant argues that the rational basis for belief in God and immortality rests in morality, rather than in theoretical proofs or in an inference to be drawn from our observation of the apparent design in nature. The most detailed account of his argument appears in Part One, Book Two, the "Dialectic," of the *Critique of Practical Reason*. In *Religion within the Boundaries of Mere Reason* and in his class lectures on philosophical theology (available in *Religion and Rational Theology*, in the Cambridge Edition of the Works of Immanuel Kant, Cambridge University Press, 1996), Kant also explores the rational roots of some of the more particular ideas of religion, such as atonement, salvation, grace, miracles, and the need for a church. In a similar way, the *Metaphysical First Principles of the Doctrine of Right* explores the rational roots of concepts used in the Roman and European legal traditions, such as the concept of a right and of the social contract.

The other reason for attention to religion and politics springs from Kant's conviction that the committed moral agent has a deep need to place faith in some vision of how the kingdom of ends may actually be realized. In the three *Critiques* and in *Religion within the Boundaries of Mere Reason*, Kant explains how this need may legitimately lead us to hope that there is a moral deity and an afterlife. But Kant also explored the possibility of a more secular faith whose object is the inevitable progress of history towards the realization of the good. Kant touches on this last idea at the very end of the *Metaphysical First Principles of the Doctrine of Right* (6:354–355), and spells it out in more detail in some of his essays on history, especially "Idea for a Universal History with a Cosmopolitan Aim," "Toward Perpetual Peace," and "An Old Question Raised Again: Is the Human Race Constantly Progressing?" (All of these may be found in *Kant: Political Writings*, trans. H. B. Nisbet, ed. Hans Reiss, 2nd edn., Cambridge University Press, 1991.)

The secondary literature on Kant's ethics in general and the *Groundwork* in particular is vast. Until recently, a disproportionately large part of it was provoked by Hegel's famous contention that Kant's Formula of Universal Law is "empty" (see *Elements of the Philosophy of Right* [1821], trans. H. B. Nisbet, ed. Allen W. Wood, Cambridge University Press, 1991). One of the best discussions of the universalization test is to be found in the two chapters devoted to Kant in Marcus Singer's *Generalization in Ethics* (New York: Atheneum, 1961). Another important discussion is found in Onora Nell (O'Neill), *Acting on Principle: An Essay on Kantian Ethics* (New York: Columbia University Press, 1975).

In the middle years of the twentieth century people studied Kant's ethics with the aid of H. J. Paton's *The Categorical Imperative: A Study in Kant's Moral Philosophy* (London: Hutchinson & Co., 1947; later reprinted University of Chicago Press, 1948, and Philadelphia: University of Pennsylvania Press, 1971) and Lewis White Beck's *A Commentary on Kant's Critique of Practical Reason* (University of Chicago Press, 1960). Roger Sullivan's *Immanuel Kant's Moral Theory* (Cambridge University Press, 1989) was one of the first attempts to deal with Kant's ethical theory as a whole and contains an extensive and useful bibliography of work done up until that time. For a more recent commentary on the *Groundwork*, see Jens Timmermann, *Kant's Groundwork of the Metaphysics of Morals: A Commentary* (Cambridge University Press, 2007).

Interest in Kant's ethics has been lively during the last few decades, which have produced a number of collections of essays or books in which the interpretation and reconstruction of the Kantian texts serves as the background to philosophical defenses of his theory. See for instance, Stephen Engstrom, *The Form of Practical Knowledge: A Study of the Categorical Imperative* (Cambridge, MA: Harvard University Press, 2009); Barbara Herman, *The Practice of Moral Judgment* (Cambridge, MA: Harvard University Press, 1993) and *Moral Literacy* (Cambridge, MA: Harvard University Press, 2007); Thomas Hill, Jr., *Autonomy and Self-Respect* (Cambridge University Press, 1991); *Dignity and Practical Reason in Kant's Moral Theory* (Ithaca: Cornell University Press, 1992); *Respect, Pluralism, and Justice* (Oxford University Press, 2000); and *Human Welfare and Moral Worth: Kantian Perspectives* (Oxford University Press, 2002); Christine M. Korsgaard, *Creating the Kingdom of Ends* (Cambridge University Press, 1996), and some of the essays in *The Constitution of Agency* (Oxford University Press, 2008); Onora O'Neill, *Constructions of Reason* (Cambridge University Press, 1989); Andrews Reath, *Agency and Autonomy in Kant's Moral Theory* (Oxford University Press, 2006); and Allen W. Wood, *Kant's Ethical Thought* (Cambridge University Press, 1999) and *Kantian Ethics* (Cambridge University Press, 2007).

The practical implications of Kant's theory, sometimes for moral issues which Kant himself never had occasion to consider, have also received attention during this period. Thomas Hill, Jr., considers such issues as affirmative action, our treatment of the environment, and terrorism in *Autonomy and Self-Respect* and *Dignity and Practical Reason*. Christine Korsgaard defends a Kantian conception of duties to other animals in "Fellow Creatures: Kantian Ethics and Our Duties to Animals" (in *The Tanner Lectures on Human Values*, Volume 25, ed. Grethe B. Peterson, Salt Lake City: University of Utah Press, 2005 and on the web at: www.tannerlectures.utah.edu/lectures/documents/volume25/korsgaard_2005.pdf). Onora O'Neill applies Kantian concepts to the problem of famine in *Faces of Hunger* (London: Allen & Unwin, 1986).

Another topic of particular interest in recent years has been the relationship between Kantian and Aristotelian ethics, with many philosophers eager to challenge the received view that these two approaches are inimical to each other. These ideas are explored in *Aristotle, Kant, and the Stoics: Rethinking Happiness and Duty* (ed. Stephen Engstrom and Jennifer Whiting, Cambridge University Press, 1996) and in Nancy Sherman's *Making a Necessity of Virtue: Aristotle and Kant on Virtue* (Cambridge University Press, 1997). A number of essays arguing for common themes in the work of Kant, Plato, and Aristotle appear in

Christine Korsgaard's *The Constitution of Agency* (Oxford University Press, 2008).

The flourishing state of work on Kant's ethics at present owes a great deal to the teaching of John Rawls, who lectured regularly on Kant's ethical theory at Harvard. Some of his lectures on Kant and other major philosophers of the tradition can be found in *Lectures on the History of Moral Philosophy* (Cambridge, MA: Harvard University Press, 2000). Rawls's own influential political theory in *A Theory of Justice* (Cambridge, MA: Harvard University Press, 1971) and *Political Liberalism* (New York: Columbia University Press, 1993) is strongly influenced by Kant's moral theory. Apart from the lectures, Rawls himself published only one essay directly about Kant, "Themes in Kant's Moral Philosophy" (in Eckart Förster, ed., *Kant's Transcendental Deductions*, Stanford University Press, 1989; reprinted in *John Rawls: Collected Papers* [Cambridge, MA: Harvard University Press, 1999]). But quite a few contemporary defenders of Kant studied with Rawls. *Reclaiming the History of Ethics: Essays for John Rawls* (ed. Andrews Reath, Barbara Herman, and Christine M. Korsgaard, Cambridge University Press, 1997), a collection of essays assembled in Rawls's honor by his former students, includes eight essays primarily devoted to Kant.

Rawls is not the only contemporary philosopher whose work on ethics and politics has been inspired by Kant's, and the reader may wish to explore what other philosophers have done with Kantian ideas in the construction of their own views. Examples include Stephen Darwall, *Impartial Reason* (Ithaca: Cornell University Press, 1983) and *The Second-Person Standpoint* (Cambridge, MA: Harvard University Press, 2009); Alan Donagan, *The Theory of Morality* (University of Chicago Press, 1977); Alan Gewirth, *Reason and Morality* (University of Chicago Press, 1978); Christine M. Korsgaard, *The Sources of Normativity* (Cambridge University Press, 1996) and *Self-Constitution: Agency, Identity and Integrity* (Oxford University Press, 2009); Thomas Nagel, *The Possibility of Altruism* (Oxford: Clarendon Press, 1970 and Princeton University Press, 1978); and Onora O'Neill, *Towards Justice and Virtue* (Cambridge University Press, 1996). Kant's impact on moral philosophy remains pervasive and profound.

Groundwork of the Metaphysics of Morals

Preface

Ancient Greek philosophy was divided into three sciences: **physics**, **ethics**, and **logic**.[1] This division is perfectly suitable to the nature of the matter, and there is no need to amend it, except perhaps just to add its principle, partly so as to assure oneself in this way of its completeness, partly to be able to determine correctly the necessary subdivisions.

All rational cognition is either *material* and considers some object, or *formal* and occupied merely with the form of the understanding and of reason itself, and with the universal rules of thinking as such, regardless of differences among its objects. Formal philosophy is called **logic**, whereas material philosophy, which has to do with determinate objects and the laws to which they are subject, is once again twofold. For these laws are either laws of *nature*, or of *freedom*. The science of the first is called **physics**, that of the other is **ethics**; the former is also called doctrine of nature, the latter doctrine of morals.

Logic can have no empirical part, i.e. one in which the universal and necessary laws of thinking would rest on grounds taken from experience; for in that case it would not be logic, i.e. a canon for the understanding, or for reason, that holds and must be demonstrated in all thinking. By contrast, natural as well as moral philosophy can each have its empirical part, since the former must determine the laws for nature, as an object of experience, the latter for the human being's will, in so far as it is affected by nature, the first as laws according to which everything happens, the second as those according to which everything ought to happen, while still taking into consideration the conditions under which quite often it does not happen.

All philosophy in so far as it is based on grounds of experience can be called *empirical*, that which presents its doctrines solely from a priori principles *pure* philosophy. The latter, if it is merely formal, is called *logic*; but if it is limited to determinate objects of the understanding it is called *metaphysics*.

In this way there arises the idea of a twofold metaphysics, a *metaphysics of nature* and a *metaphysics of morals*. Physics will thus have its empirical, but also a rational part; so too will ethics, though here the empirical part might in particular be called *practical anthropology*, the rational part actually *moral science*.[a]

All professions, crafts, and arts have gained by the distribution of labor, namely when one person does not do everything, but each limits himself to a certain task that differs noticeably from others in the way it is carried out, so as to be able to accomplish it most perfectly and with greater ease.[2] Where labor is not differentiated and distributed like that, where everyone is a jack-of-all-trades, professions still remain in a most barbarous state. It would by itself be an object not unworthy of consideration to ask: whether pure philosophy in all its parts might not require its own specialist, and whether the learned profession as a whole might not be better off if those who, conforming to the taste of their public, are in the habit of peddling the empirical mixed with the rational in all sorts of proportions unknown to themselves – who call themselves independent thinkers, but others, who prepare the merely rational part, ponderers – were warned not to pursue two occupations at once that are very dissimilar in the way they are to be carried out, for each of which a special talent is perhaps required, and which united in one person produce only bunglers. But here I just ask whether the nature of the science might not require that the empirical part always be carefully separated from the rational, and that actual (empirical) physics be prefaced by a metaphysics of nature, and practical anthropology by a metaphysics of morals, which would have to be carefully cleansed of everything empirical; so that we may know how 4:389 much pure reason can accomplish in both cases, and from what sources it draws by itself this peculiar a priori instruction, whether the latter business be pursued by all teachers of morals (whose name is legion) or only by some, who feel a calling to it.

Since here my purpose is actually directed towards moral philosophy, I limit the question presented just to this: is it not thought to be of the utmost necessity to work out for once a pure moral philosophy,

[a] *Moral*, a word used in the eighteenth century for the systematic study of morality, not for morality itself (*Sittlichkeit*, *Moralität*) or morals (*Sitten*).

completely cleansed of everything that might be in some way empirical and belongs to anthropology? For that there must be such is of itself clear from the common idea of duty and of moral laws. Everyone must admit that a law, if it is to hold morally, i.e. as the ground of an obligation, must carry with it absolute necessity; that the command: thou shalt not lie, does not just hold for human beings only, as if other rational beings did not have to heed it; and so with all remaining actual moral laws; hence that the ground of the obligation here must not be sought in the nature of the human being, or in the circumstances of the world in which he is placed, but a priori solely in concepts of pure reason, and that any other prescription that is founded on principles of mere experience – and even a prescription that is in some certain respect universal, in so far as it relies in the least part on empirical grounds, perhaps just for a motivating ground – can indeed be called a practical rule, but never a moral law.

Thus not only do moral laws, along with their principles, differ essentially in practical cognition from all the rest, in which there is something empirical,[b] but all moral philosophy rests entirely on its pure part and, applied to the human being, it does not borrow the least thing from our acquaintance with him (anthropology), but gives him, as a rational being, laws a priori; which of course still require a power of judgment sharpened by experience, partly to distinguish in what cases they are applicable, partly to obtain for them access[c] to the will of a human being and momentum for performance, since he, as himself affected by so many inclinations, is indeed capable of the idea of a practical pure reason, but not so easily able to make it effective in concreto[d] in the conduct of his life.

A metaphysics of morals is thus indispensably necessary, not merely on the grounds of speculation, for investigating the source of the practical principles[e] that lie a priori in our reason, but because morals themselves remain subject to all sorts of corruption as long as we lack that guideline and supreme norm by which to judge them correctly. For in the case of what is to be morally good it is not enough that it *conform* with the moral

4:390

---

[b] Here, as elsewhere, differences between German and English punctuation create difficulties. It is not altogether clear from the context whether the clause "in which ... empirical" is restrictive or non-restrictive.

[c] or "admission" (of laws, doctrines, or theories, to the will of an agent) by means of moral instruction

[d] tangibly, palpably; not abstract

[e] Kant does not consistently distinguish between *Grundsatz* and *Prinzip*. Both have been translated as "principle."

law, but it must also be done *for its sake*; if not, that conformity is only very contingent and precarious, because the immoral ground[f] will indeed now and then produce actions that conform with the law, but in many cases actions that are contrary to it. But now the moral law in its purity and genuineness (which in practical matters is of the greatest significance) is to be sought nowhere else than in a pure philosophy; it (metaphysics) must thus come first, and without it there can be no moral philosophy at all; and that which mixes these pure principles in with empirical ones does not even deserve the name of a philosophy (which after all is distinguished from common rational cognition in that it presents in a separate science what the latter comprehends only as intermingled with other things), much less that of a moral philosophy, since it even infringes on the purity of morals themselves by this intermingling and proceeds contrary to its own end.

However, let it not be thought that what is here called for already exists in the guise of the propaedeutic[g] of the famous *Wolff* for his moral philosophy, namely that which he called *Universal Practical Philosophy*, and that we do not therefore have to open up an entirely new field.[3] Precisely because it was to be a universal practical philosophy it took into consideration not a will of any particular kind – such as one that is completely determined from a priori principles, without any empirical motivating grounds, and could be called a pure will – but rather willing generally, with all actions and conditions that belong to it in this general sense; and in that it differs from a metaphysics of morals, in just the way that general logic differs from transcendental philosophy, the first of which presents actions and rules of thinking *in general*, the latter the particular actions and rules of **pure** thinking, i.e. of that by which objects are cognized completely a priori. For the metaphysics of morals is to investigate the idea and the principles of a possible *pure* will, and not the actions and conditions of human willing in general, which are largely drawn from psychology. The fact that (though contrary to all warrant) there is also talk of moral laws and duties in this universal practical philosophy constitutes no objection to my assertion. For the authors of that science remain true to their idea of it in this too: they do not distinguish motivating grounds that, as such, are represented completely a priori by reason alone and are actually moral, from empirical ones, which the understanding elevates to general concepts

4:391

---

[f] *der unsittliche Grund*; "non-moral" is probably too weak   [g] a preliminary or introductory work

merely by comparing experiences, but they consider them, without attending to the difference of their sources, only in terms of their greater or lesser sum (as they are all viewed as being of the same kind), and thereby form their concept of *obligation*, which of course is anything but moral, but is still such as can only be demanded in a philosophy that never passes judgment on the *origin* of all possible practical concepts, whether they really take place a priori or merely a posteriori.

Intending, then, to publish some day a Metaphysics of Morals, I issue this Groundwork in advance.[4] Indeed, there is actually no foundation for it other than the Critique of a *pure practical reason*,[5] just as for metaphysics there is the Critique of pure speculative reason already published.[6] But in part the former is not of such utmost necessity as the latter, since human reason, even in the commonest understanding, can easily be brought to a high measure of correctness and accuracy in moral matters, whereas in its theoretical but pure use it is totally and entirely dialectical; in part I require that the critique of a pure practical reason, if it is to be complete, also be able to present its unity with speculative reason[h] in a common principle; because in the end there can be only one and the same reason, which must differ merely in its application. However, I could not yet bring it to such completeness here without introducing considerations of a wholly different kind and confusing the reader. On account of this I have availed myself of the label of a *Groundwork of the Metaphysics of Morals*, and not of a *Critique of Pure Practical Reason* instead.

But since, thirdly, a Metaphysics of Morals, regardless of its daunting title, is still capable of a great degree of popularity and suitability for the common understanding, I find it useful to separate from it this preparatory work of laying its foundation, so that I may omit the subtleties it 4:392 unavoidably contains from more accessible doctrines in the future.

The present groundwork, however, is nothing more than the identification and corroboration *of the supreme principle of morality*, which by itself constitutes a business that is complete in its purpose and to be separated from every other moral investigation. My assertions – about this principal question, which is important and has until now been far from satisfactorily discussed – would indeed receive much light from the application of that principle to the entire system, and great confirmation from the adequacy that it exhibits everywhere; but I had to forgo this

---

[h] or "unity with the critique of speculative reason," as indicated by the first edition

advantage, which would also fundamentally be more self-gratifying than in the general interest, since the ease with which a principle can be used and its apparent adequacy yields no wholly reliable proof of its correctness, but rather arouses a certain partiality against investigating and weighing it in all strictness by itself, regardless of the consequence.

In this work, I have adopted the method that is, I believe, most fitting if one wants to take one's route analytically from common cognition to the determination of its supreme principle and in turn synthetically from the examination of this principle and its sources back to common cognition, in which we find it used. That is why it is divided as follows:

1. *First section:* Transition from common to philosophical moral rational cognition.
2. *Second section:* Transition from popular moral philosophy to the metaphysics of morals.
3. *Third section:* Final step from the metaphysics of morals to the critique of pure practical reason.

First section

Transition from common to philosophical moral rational cognition

It is impossible to think of anything at all in the world, or indeed even beyond it, that could be taken to be good without limitation, except a **good will**. Understanding, wit, judgment, and whatever else the *talents* of the mind may be called, or confidence, resolve, and persistency of intent, as qualities of *temperament*, are no doubt in many respects good and desirable; but they can also be extremely evil and harmful if the will that is to make use of these gifts of nature, and whose distinctive constitution is therefore called *character*, is not good. It is just the same with *gifts of fortune*. Power, riches, honor, even health, and the entire well-being and contentment with one's condition, under the name of *happiness*, inspire confidence and thereby quite often overconfidence as well, unless a good will is present to correct and make generally purposive[i] their influence on the mind, and with it also the whole principle for acting; not to mention that a rational impartial spectator can nevermore take any delight in the sight of the uninterrupted prosperity of a being adorned with no feature of a pure and good will, and that a good will thus appears to constitute the indispensable condition even of the worthiness to be happy.

Some qualities are even conducive to this good will itself and can make its work much easier; but regardless of this they have no inner uncondi- tional worth, but always presuppose a good will, which limits the high esteem in which they are otherwise rightly held, and makes it impermissible

---

[i] *allgemein-zweckmäßig*; alternatively "universally purposive," a tricky expression not used elsewhere in the *Groundwork*

to take them for good per se. Moderation in affects and passions, self-control and sober deliberation are not only good in many respects, they even appear to constitute part of the *inner* worth of a person; but they are far from deserving to be declared good without limitation (however unconditionally they were praised by the ancients). For without principles of a good will they can become most evil, and the cold blood of a scoundrel makes him not only far more dangerous, but also immediately more loathsome in our eyes than he would have been taken to be without it.

A good will is good not because of what it effects, or accomplishes, not because of its fitness to attain some intended end, but good just by its willing, i.e. in itself; and, considered by itself, it is to be esteemed beyond compare much higher than anything that could ever be brought about by it in favor of some inclination, and indeed, if you will, the sum of all inclinations. Even if by some particular disfavor of fate, or by the scanty endowment of a stepmotherly nature, this will should entirely lack the capacity to carry through its purpose; if despite its greatest striving it should still accomplish nothing, and only the good will were to remain (not, of course, as a mere wish, but as the summoning of all means that are within our control); then, like a jewel, it would still shine by itself, as something that has its full worth in itself. Usefulness or fruitlessness can neither add anything to this worth, nor take anything away from it. It would, as it were, be only the setting to enable us to handle it better in ordinary commerce, or to attract the attention of those who are not yet expert enough; but not to recommend it to experts, or to determine its worth.

Even so, in this idea of the absolute worth of a mere will, not taking into account any utility in its estimation, there is something so strange that, regardless of all the agreement with it even of common reason, a suspicion must yet arise that it might perhaps covertly be founded merely on some high-flown fantastication, and that we may have misunderstood Nature's[j] 4:395 purpose in assigning Reason to our will as its ruler. We shall therefore submit this idea to examination from this point of view.

In the natural predispositions of an organized being, i.e. one arranged purposively[k] for life, we assume as a principle that no organ will be found in

---

[j] Nature, Reason, Philosophy, and Virtue are occasionally capitalized, and referred to with the feminine pronoun, to indicate that Kant is using these words allegorically. Allegorical and literal passages are not always easy to distinguish.

[k] *Zweck* is translated as "end" except when it occurs as part of *zweckmäßig* ("purposive") or *zwecklos* ("purposeless").

it for any end that is not also the most fitting for it and the most suitable. Now in a being that has reason and a will, if the actual end of Nature were its *preservation*, its *prosperity*, in a word its *happiness*, then she would have made very bad arrangements for this in appointing the creature's Reason as the accomplisher of this purpose. For all the actions that it has to perform with a view to this purpose, and the whole rule of its conduct, would be marked out for it far more accurately by instinct, and that end would thereby have been obtained much more reliably than can ever be done by reason; and if in addition reason should have been bestowed on the favored creature, it would have had to serve it only to contemplate the fortunate predisposition of its nature, to admire it, to rejoice in it, and to be grateful for it to the beneficent cause; but not to subject its desiderative faculty[1] to that weak and deceptive guidance and meddle with Nature's purpose; in a word, Nature would have prevented Reason from striking out into *practical use*, and from having the impudence, with its feeble insights, to devise its own plan for happiness and for the means of achieving it. Nature herself would have taken over the choice not only of ends, but also of means, and as a wise precaution would have entrusted them both solely to instinct.

In actual fact, we do find that the more a cultivated reason engages with the purpose of enjoying life and with happiness, so much the further does a human being stray from true contentment; and from this there arises in many, and indeed in those who are most experienced in its use, if only they are sincere enough to admit it, a certain degree of *misology*, i.e. hatred of reason, since after calculating all the advantages they derive – I do not say from the invention of all the arts of common luxury, but even from the sciences (which in the end also appear to them to be a luxury of the understanding) – they still find that they have in fact just brought more hardship upon their shoulders than they have gained in happiness, and 4:396 that because of this they eventually envy, rather than disdain, the more common run of people, who are closer to the guidance of mere natural instinct, and who do not allow their reason much influence on their behavior. And to that extent one must admit that the judgment of those who greatly moderate and even reduce below zero the vainglorious eulogies extolling the advantages that reason was supposed to obtain for us with regard to the happiness and contentment of life, is by no means

---

[1] *Begehrungsvermögen*. For Kant's definition of this term cf. the *Critique of Practical Reason* (5:8 n.) and the *Metaphysics of Morals* (6:211). In human beings, the desiderative faculty is the will.

sullen, or ungrateful to the kindliness of the government of the world; but that these judgments are covertly founded on the idea of another and far worthier purpose of their existence, to which, and not to happiness, reason is quite properly destined, and to which, as its supreme condition, the private purpose of a human being must therefore largely take second place.

For since reason is not sufficiently fit to guide the will reliably with regard to its objects and the satisfaction of all our needs (which in part it does itself multiply) – an end to which an implanted natural instinct would have led much more reliably – but reason as a practical faculty, i.e. as one that is meant to influence the *will*, has yet been imparted to us, its true function[m] must be to produce a *will that is good*, not for other purposes *as a means*, but good *in itself* – for which reason was absolutely necessary – since nature has everywhere else gone to work purposively in distributing its predispositions. Therefore this will need not, indeed, be the only and the entire good, but it must yet be the highest good, and the condition of everything else, even of all longing for happiness; in which case it is quite consistent with the wisdom of nature when one perceives that the cultivation of reason, which is required for the first and unconditional purpose, in many ways limits – at least in this life – the attainment of the second, namely of happiness, which is always conditional, indeed that it may reduce it to less than nothing without nature's proceeding unpurposively in this; because reason, which recognizes as its highest practical function the grounding of a good will, in attaining this purpose, is capable only of a contentment after its own kind, namely from fulfilling an end that again is determined only by reason, even if this should involve much infringement on the ends of inclination.

4:397 In order, then, to unravel[n] the concept of a will to be highly esteemed in itself and good apart from any further purpose, as it already dwells in natural sound understanding and needs not so much to be taught as rather just to be brought to light,[o] this concept that always comes first in estimating the entire worth of our actions and constitutes the condition of everything else: we shall inspect the concept of **duty**, which contains that of a good will, though under certain subjective limitations and

---

[m] or "vocation" (Gregor), in the context of teleology; *Bestimmung* has been rendered "determination" elsewhere

[n] *entwickeln*; or perhaps "explicate" (Gregor)

[o] *aufgeklärt*; the usual English translation "clarified" obscures the connection with the project of the Enlightenment (*Aufklärung*)

hindrances, which, however, far from concealing it and making it unrecognizable, rather bring it out by contrast and make it shine forth all the more brightly.

I here pass over all actions already recognized as contrary to duty, even though they may be useful in this or that respect; for in their case there is no question whether they might have been done *from duty*, since they even conflict with it. I also set aside actions that actually conform with duty but to which human beings immediately have *no inclination*, but which they still perform, because they are impelled to do so by another inclination. For there it is easy to distinguish whether the action that conforms with duty was done *from duty* or from a self-serving purpose. It is much more difficult to notice this difference when an action conforms with duty and the subject has in addition an *immediate* inclination towards it. E.g. it certainly conforms with duty that a shopkeeper not overcharge his inexperienced customer, and where there is much commerce, a prudent merchant actually does not do this, but keeps a fixed general price for everyone, so that a child may buy from him just as well as everyone else. Thus one is served *honestly*; but this is not nearly enough for us to believe that the merchant proceeded in this way from duty and principles of honesty; his advantage required it; it cannot be assumed here that he had, besides, an immediate inclination towards his customers, so as from love, as it were, to give no one preference over another in the matter of price. Thus the action was done neither from duty, nor from immediate inclination, but merely for a self-interested purpose.

By contrast, to preserve one's life is one's duty,[p] and besides everyone has an immediate inclination to do so. But on account of this the often anxious care with which the greatest part of humanity attends to it has yet no inner worth, and their maxim no moral content. They preserve their lives *in* 4:398 *conformity with duty*, but not *from duty*. By contrast, if adversities and hopeless grief have entirely taken away the taste for life; if the unfortunate man, strong of soul, more indignant about his fate than despondent or dejected, wishes for death, and yet preserves his life, without loving it, not from inclination, or fear, but from duty; then his maxim has a moral content.

To be beneficent where one can is one's duty, and besides there are many souls so attuned to compassion that, even without another motivating

---

[p] The standard translation is "is a duty," but when Kant uses the expression *ist Pflicht* he does not mean to say that there is, as such, a specific duty to do something, but simply that a certain action is obligatory (that one has to do it).

ground of vanity, or self-interest, they find an inner gratification in spreading joy around them, and can relish the contentment of others, in so far as it is their work. But I assert that in such a case an action of this kind – however much it conforms with duty, however amiable it may be – still has no true moral worth, but stands on the same footing as other inclinations, e.g. the inclination to honor, which if it fortunately lights upon what is in fact in the general interest and in conformity with duty, and hence honorable, deserves praise and encouragement, but not high esteem; for the maxim lacks moral content, namely to do such actions not from inclination, but *from duty*. Suppose, then, that the mind of that friend of humanity were beclouded by his own grief, which extinguishes all compassion for the fate of others; that he still had the means to benefit others in need, but the need of others did not touch him because he is sufficiently occupied with his own; and that now, as inclination no longer stimulates him to it, he were yet to tear himself out of this deadly insensibility, and to do the action without any inclination, solely from duty; not until then does it have its genuine moral worth. Still further: if nature had as such placed little sympathy in the heart of this or that man; if (otherwise honest) he were by temperament cold and indifferent to the sufferings of others, perhaps because he himself is equipped with the peculiar gift of patience and enduring strength towards his own, and presupposes, or even requires, the same in every other; if nature had not actually formed such a man (who would truly not be its worst product) to be a friend of humanity, would he not still find within himself a source from which to give himself a far higher worth than that of a good-natured temperament may be? Certainly! It is just there that the worth of

4:399 character commences, which is moral and beyond all comparison the highest, namely that he be beneficent, not from inclination, but from duty.

To secure one's own happiness is one's duty (at least indirectly); for lack of contentment with one's condition, in the trouble of many worries and amidst unsatisfied needs, could easily become a great *temptation to transgress one's duties*. But, even without taking note of duty, all human beings have already of their own the most powerful and intimate inclination to happiness, as it is just in this idea that all inclinations unite in one sum. However, the prescription of happiness is predominantly such, that it greatly infringes on some inclinations and yet human beings can form no determinate and reliable concept of the sum of the satisfaction of all under the name of happiness; which is why it is not surprising that a single inclination – if determinate with regard to what it promises, and to the time its satisfaction can be obtained[q] – can outweigh a wavering idea, and that a human being, e.g. someone suffering from gout of the foot, can choose to enjoy what he fancies and to suffer what he can since, according to his calculation, at least then he has not denied himself the enjoyment of the present moment because of perhaps groundless expectations of some good fortune that is meant to lie in health. But also in this case, if the universal inclination to happiness did not determine his will, if health, at least for him, did not enter into this calculation so necessarily, then here, as in all other cases, there still remains a law, namely to advance one's happiness,[r] not from inclination, but from duty; and it is not until then that his conduct has its actual moral worth.

It is in this way, no doubt, that we are to understand the passages from Scripture that contain the command to love one's neighbor, even our enemy.[7] For love as inclination cannot be commanded, but beneficence from duty itself – even if no inclination whatsoever impels us to it, indeed if natural and unconquerable aversion resists – is *practical* and not *pathological*[s] love, which lies in the will and not in the propensity of sensation, in principles of action and not in melting compassion; and only the former can be commanded.

The second proposition[8] is: an action from duty has its moral worth *not in the purpose* that is to be attained by it, but in the maxim according to which it is resolved upon,[t] and thus it does not depend on the actuality of the object of the action, but merely on the *principle* of *willing* according to which – regardless of any object of the desiderative faculty – the action is done. That the purposes that we may have when we act, and their effects, as ends and incentives[u] of the will, can bestow on actions no unconditional and moral worth, is clear from what was previously said. In what, then, can this worth lie, if it is not to consist in the will with reference to their hoped-for effect? It can lie nowhere else *than in the principle of the will*, regardless of the ends that can be effected by such action; for the will

4:400

---

[q] alternatively "sustained," but Kant's usage elsewhere appears to imply the translation adopted here

[r] or possibly "his happiness" (Gregor), but the command should probably be formulated impersonally, as at the beginning of this paragraph

[s] love belonging to the passive, sensuous side of human nature, as opposed to reason; not used by Kant in the sense of morbid or obsessive

[t] "but in ... resolved upon" is an addition of the second edition

[u] Gregor's term, now widely accepted, has been retained although it may seem to suggest some external thing that initiates motivation, rather than the internal "spring" or "drive" that Kant had in mind. Kantian "incentives" are motivating desires that propel the agent forward if he or she so decides. A *Triebfeder* is the mainspring of motion, as in a clock or an old-fashioned tin toy.

stands halfway between its a priori principle, which is formal, and its a posteriori incentive, which is material, as it were at a crossroads, and since it must after all be determined by something, it will have to be determined by the formal principle of willing as such when an action is done from duty, as every material principle has been taken away from it.

The third proposition, as the conclusion from both previous ones, I would express as follows: *duty is the necessity of an action from respect*^{v} *for the law*. For the object as the effect of the action I have in mind I can indeed have *inclination*, but *never respect*, precisely because it is merely an effect and not activity of a will.^{w} Likewise, I cannot have respect for inclination as such, whether it is mine or that of another; I can at most in the first case approve of it, in the second at times love it myself, i.e. view it as favorable to my own advantage. Only what is connected with my will merely as ground, never as effect, what does not serve my inclination, but outweighs it, or at least excludes it entirely from calculations when we make a choice, hence the mere law by itself, can be an object of respect and thus a command. Now, an action from duty is to separate off entirely the influence of inclination, and with it every object of the will; thus nothing remains for the will that could determine it except, objectively, the *law* and, subjectively, *pure respect* for this practical law, and hence the maxim*
4:401 of complying with such a law, even if it infringes on all my inclinations.

Thus the moral worth of the action does not lie in the effect that is expected from it, nor therefore in any principle of action that needs to borrow its motivating ground from this expected effect. For all these effects (agreeableness of one's condition, indeed even advancement of the happiness of others) could also have been brought about by other causes, and thus there was, for this, no need of the will of a rational being; even so, in it alone can the highest and unconditional good be found. Nothing other than the *representation of the law* in itself – *which of course can take place only in a rational being* – in so far as it, not the hoped-for effect, is the determining ground of the will, can therefore constitute the pre-eminent

---

* A *maxim* is the subjective principle of willing; the objective principle (i.e. the one that would also subjectively serve all rational beings as the practical principle if reason had complete control over the desiderative faculty) is the practical *law*.

^{v} H. J. Paton's "reverence" is in some ways a more natural word for a positive motivating moral force like Kantian *Achtung*; but "respect" is now generally used in discussions of Kantian ethics, and it has the additional advantage of resonating with readers beyond the world of Kant scholarship.

^{w} Second edition; the first edition has "effect of my will"

good that we call moral, which is already present in the person himself who acts according to it, and is not first to be expected from the effect.*

But what kind of law can that possibly be, the representation of which – 4:402 even without regard for the effect expected from it – must determine the will for it to be called good absolutely and without limitation? Since I have robbed the will of all impulses that could arise for it from following some particular law, nothing remains but as such the universal conformity of actions with law, which alone is to serve the will as its principle, i.e. I ought never to proceed except in such a way *that I could also will that my maxim should become a universal law.* Here, then, mere conformity with law as such (not founded on any law determined with a view to certain actions) is what serves the will as its principle, and must so serve it if duty is not to be as such an empty delusion and a chimerical concept; common human reason in its practical judging is actually in perfect agreement with this, and always has the envisaged principle before its eyes.

Let the question be, e.g., may I not, when I am in trouble, make a promise with the intention not to keep it? Here I easily discern the different meanings the question can have: whether it is prudent, or whether it conforms with duty to make a false promise. The former can no doubt quite often take place. I do see very well that it is not enough to extricate myself from the present predicament by means of this subterfuge, but that it requires careful deliberation whether this lie may not later give rise to much greater inconvenience for me than those from which I am now

---

* I might be accused of using the word *respect* just to seek refuge in an obscure feeling, instead of giving distinct information about the matter in question by means of a concept of reason. But even though respect is a feeling, it is not one *received* by influence, but one *self-wrought* by a rational concept and therefore specifically different from all feelings of the former kind, which come down to inclination or fear. What I recognize immediately as a law for myself I recognize with respect, which signifies merely the consciousness of the *subordination* of my will to a law, without mediation of other influences on my sense. The immediate determination of the will by the law and the consciousness of this is called *respect*, so that it is viewed as the *effect* of the law on the subject and not as its *cause*. Respect is actually the representation of a worth that infringes on my self-love. Thus it is something that is considered an object neither of inclination, nor of fear, even though it is at the same time somewhat analogous to both. The *object* of respect is therefore solely the *law*, the one that we impose upon *ourselves* and yet as in itself necessary. As a law we are subject to it, without consulting self-love; as imposed upon us by ourselves, it is yet a consequence of our will, and in the first regard it has an analogy with fear, in the second with inclination. All respect for a person is actually only respect for the law (of righteousness etc.) of which he gives us the example. Because we also view expanding our talents as our duty, we represent a person of talents also, as it were, as the *example of a law* (to become like him in this by practice)ˣ and this is what constitutes our respect. All moral *interest*, so called, consists solely in *respect* for the law.

ˣ This parenthetical remark is an addition of the second edition.

liberating myself; and – since with all my supposed *cunning* the consequences cannot be so easily foreseen that trust once lost might not be far more disadvantageous to me than any ill that I now mean to avoid – whether one might not act *more prudently* in this matter by proceeding according to a universal[y] maxim, and by making it one's habit to promise nothing except with the intention of keeping it. But here it soon becomes clear to me that such a maxim will still only be founded on the dreaded consequences. Now, to be truthful from duty is something quite different from being truthful from dread of adverse consequences; as in the first case, the concept of the action in itself already contains a law for me, whereas in the second I must first look around elsewhere to see what effects on me this might involve. For if I deviate from the principle of duty, this is quite certainly evil; but

4:403 if I defect from my maxim of prudence, that can sometimes be very advantageous to me, though it is of course safer to adhere to it. However, to instruct myself in the very quickest and yet undeceptive[z] way with regard to responding to this problem – whether a lying promise conforms with duty – I ask myself: would I actually be content that my maxim (to extricate myself from a predicament by means of an untruthful promise) should hold as a universal law (for myself as well as for others), and would I be able to say to myself: everyone may make an untruthful promise when he finds himself in a predicament from which he can extricate himself in no other way? Then I soon become aware that I could indeed will the lie, but by no means a universal law to lie; for according to such a law there would actually be no promise at all, since it would be futile to pretend my will to others with regard to my future actions, who would not believe this pretense; or, if they rashly did so, would pay me back in like coin, and hence my maxim, as soon as it were made a universal law, would have to destroy itself.

I do not, therefore, need any wide-ranging acuteness to see what I have to do for my willing to be morally good. Inexperienced with regard to the course of the world, incapable of bracing myself for whatever might come to pass in it, I just ask myself: can you also will that your maxim become a universal law? If not, then it must be rejected, and that not because of some disadvantage to you, or to others, that might result, but because it cannot fit as a principle into a possible universal legislation, for which reason extracts from me immediate respect; and although I do not yet *see* on what it is founded (which the philosopher may investigate), at least I do

---

[y] As so often, it is not entirely clear whether *allgemein* means "general" or "universal."
[z] *untrügliche Art*; the principle is reliable and trustworthy

understand this much: that it is an estimation of a worth that far out-weighs any worth of what is extolled by inclination, and that the necessity of my actions from *pure* respect for the practical law is that which constitutes duty, to which every other motivating ground must give way, because it is the condition of a will good *in itself*, whose worth surpasses everything.

Thus, then, we have progressed in the moral cognition of common human reason to reach its principle, which admittedly it does not think of as separated in this way in a universal form, but yet always actually has before its eyes and uses as the standard of its judging. Here it would be 4:404 easy to show how, with this compass in hand, it is very well informed in all cases that occur, to distinguish what is good, what is evil, what conforms with duty or is contrary to it, if – without in the least teaching it anything new – one only, as Socrates did, makes it aware of its own principle; and that there is thus no need of science and philosophy to know what one has to do in order to be honest and good, indeed even to be wise and virtuous.[9] It should actually have been possible to presume all along that acquaintance with what it is incumbent upon everyone to do, and hence also to know, would be the affair of every human being, even the commonest. Here one cannot without admiration observe the great advantage the practical capacity to judge has over the theoretical in common human understanding. In the latter, when common reason dares to depart from the laws of experience and the perceptions of the senses, it falls into nothing but sundry incomprehensibilities and internal contradictions, or at least into a chaos of uncertainty, obscurity, and instability. But in practical matters the power of judging first begins to show itself to advantage just when common understanding excludes all sensuous incentives from practical laws. Then it even becomes subtle, whether it seeks to engage in legalistic quibbles[a] with its conscience, or with other claims referring to what is to be called right, or seeks sincerely to determine the worth of actions for its own instruction; and, what is most important, in the latter case it stands just as good a chance of hitting the mark as a philosopher can ever expect; indeed it is almost more sure in this than even the latter, because he can have no other principle, but can easily confuse his judgment with a host of alien and irrelevant consid-erations and deflect it from the straight course. Accordingly, would it not be more advisable, in moral things, to leave it with the judgment of

---

[a] *sehikanieren*, to obstruct the claims of conscience, like a pettifogger in a law court

common reason, and at most to bring on philosophy to present the system of morals more completely and accessibly, and likewise its rules in a form more convenient for use (and still more for disputation), but not to let it lead common human understanding away from its fortunate simplicity for practical purposes, and by means of philosophy to put it on a new route of investigation and instruction?

4:405   Innocence is a glorious thing, but then again it is very sad that it is so hard to preserve and so easily seduced. Because of this even wisdom – which probably consists more in behavior than in knowledge elsewhere – yet needs science too, not in order to learn from it, but to obtain access and durability for its prescription. The human being feels within himself a powerful counterweight to all the commands of duty – which reason represents to him as so worthy of the highest respect – in his needs and inclinations, the entire satisfaction of which he sums up under the name of happiness. Now reason issues its prescriptions unrelentingly, yet without promising anything to the inclinations, and hence, as it were, with reproach and disrespect for those claims, which are so vehement and yet seem so reasonable[b] (and will not be eliminated by any command). But from this there arises a *natural dialectic*, i.e. a propensity to rationalize against those strict laws of duty, and to cast doubt on their validity, or at least their purity and strictness and, where possible, to make them better suited to our wishes and inclinations, i.e. fundamentally to corrupt them and deprive them of their entire dignity, something that in the end even common practical reason cannot endorse.

    Thus *common human reason* is impelled to leave its sphere not by some need of speculation (which never comes over it as long as it is content to be mere sound reason), but rather on practical grounds, and to take a step into the field of a *practical philosophy*, in order to receive there intelligence and distinct instruction regarding the source of this principle and its correct determination in contrast with maxims based on need and inclination, so that it may escape from the predicament caused by mutual claims, and not run the risk of being deprived of all genuine moral principles because of the ambiguity into which it easily falls. Thus also in practical common reason, when it cultivates itself, a *dialectic* inadvertently unfolds that necessitates it to seek help in philosophy, just as happens to it in its theoretical use, and the one is therefore just as unlikely as the other to find rest anywhere but in a complete critique of our reason.

            [b] or "fair"; "equitable" in a juridical context

Second section

Transition from popular moral philosophy to the metaphysics of morals

If so far we have drawn our concept of duty from the common use of our practical reason, it is by no means to be inferred from this that we have treated it as an experiential concept. Rather, if we attend to our experience of the behavior of human beings we meet frequent and, as we ourselves concede, just complaints that no reliable example can be cited of the disposition^c to act from pure duty; that, though much may be done that *conforms* with what *duty* commands, still it is always doubtful whether it is actually done *from duty* and thus has a moral worth. That is why there have been philosophers in every age who have absolutely denied the actuality of this disposition in human actions, and attributed everything to a more or less refined self-love, without however calling into doubt the correctness of the concept of morality because of this; rather, with intimate regret they made mention of the frailty and impurity of a human nature that is indeed noble enough to take an idea so worthy of respect as its prescription, but at the same time too weak to follow it, and that uses reason, which should serve it for legislation, only to take care of the interest of inclinations, whether singly or, at most, in their greatest compatibility with one another.

In fact, it is absolutely impossible by means of experience to make out 4:407 with complete certainty a single case in which the maxim of an action that otherwise conforms with duty did rest solely on moral grounds and on the

---

^c The standard translation has been retained, but it is problematic. *Gesinnung* is not just a disposition to behave in a certain way, but one's moral attitude, state of mind, conviction, or character.

representation of one's duty. For at times it is indeed the case that with the acutest self-examination we find nothing whatsoever that – besides the moral ground of duty – could have been powerful enough to move us to this or that good action and so great a sacrifice; but from this it cannot be inferred with certainty that the real determining cause of the will was not actually a covert impulse of self-love under the mere pretense of that idea; for which we then gladly flatter ourselves with the false presumption of a nobler motive, whereas in fact we can never, even by the most strenuous examination, get entirely behind our covert incentives, because when moral worth is at issue what counts is not the actions, which one sees, but their inner principles, which one does not see.

Moreover, one cannot better serve the wishes of those who ridicule all morality as the mere phantasm of a human imagination overreaching itself through self-conceit, than by conceding to them that the concepts of duty had to be drawn solely from experience (as people gladly find comfort in persuading themselves is the case with all remaining concepts as well); for then one affords them a sure triumph. From love of humanity I am willing to concede that the majority of our actions conforms with duty; but if we look more closely at the imaginations and intentions of their thoughts we everywhere come up against the dear self, which is always flashing forth, and it is on this – and not on the strict command of duty, which in many cases would require self-denial – that their purpose relies. One need not even be an enemy of virtue, but only a cold-blooded observer who does not at once take the liveliest wish for the good as its actuality, to become doubtful at certain moments (principally with advancing years and a power of judgment that experience has partly made wiser and partly more acute in observation) whether any true virtue is actually to be found in the world at all. And here nothing can protect us from falling away entirely from our ideas of duty and preserve a well-founded respect for its law in our soul, except the clear conviction that, even if there never 4:408 have been actions that have sprung from such pure sources, still, what is at issue here is not at all whether this or that does happen, but that reason by itself and independently of all appearances commands what ought to happen; and hence that actions of which the world so far has perhaps not yet given an example, and the feasibility of which might be very much doubted by someone who makes experience the foundation of everything, are still unrelentingly commanded by reason; and that e.g. pure sincerity in friendship can no less be required of everyone even if up to now there had never been a sincere friend; because this duty as a duty as such, prior to all experience, lies in the idea of a reason determining the will by a priori grounds.

If one adds that, unless one wants to refuse the concept of morality all truth and reference to some possible object, one cannot deny that its law is so extensive in its significance that it must hold not merely for human beings but for all *rational beings as such*, not merely under contingent conditions and with exceptions, but with *absolute necessity*; then it is clear that no experience can give occasion to infer even just the possibility of such apodictic laws. For by what right can we bring what is perhaps valid only under the contingent conditions of humanity into unlimited respect, as a universal prescription for every rational nature, and how shall laws of the determination of *our* will be taken as laws of the determination of the will of a rational being as such and, only as such, for our will as well, if they were merely empirical, and did not originate completely a priori from pure but practical reason?

Moreover, one could not give morality worse counsel than by seeking to borrow it from examples. For every example of it that is presented to me must itself first be judged according to principles of morality, whether it is actually worthy to serve as an original example, i.e. as a model; but by no means can it furnish the concept of it at the outset. Even the Holy One of the Gospel[d] must first be compared with our ideal of moral perfection before he is recognized as one[e]; also, he says of himself: why do you call me (whom you see) good, there is none good (the archetype of the good) but one, that is, God (whom you do not see).[10] But whence do we have the concept of God, as the highest good? Solely from the *idea* that reason a 4:409 priori devises of moral perfection, and connects inseparably with the concept of a free will. Imitation has no place at all in moral matters, and examples serve for encouragement only, i.e. they put beyond doubt the feasibility of what the law commands, they make intuitive what the practical rule expresses more generally, but they can never entitle us to set aside their true original, which lies in reason, and to go by examples.

If, then, there is no genuine supreme principle of morality that would not have to rest merely on pure reason independently of all experience, I believe it unnecessary even to ask whether it is a good thing to set forth these concepts in general (in abstracto) as they, along with the principles

---

[d] Jesus Christ   [e] as a model

23

that belong to them, are established a priori, if this cognition is to differ from common cognition and to be called philosophical. But in our age this may well be necessary. For if one were to collect votes as to what is to be preferred – pure rational cognition separated off from anything empirical, hence metaphysics of morals, or popular practical philosophy – one will soon guess on which side the preponderance^f will fall.

This condescension to popular concepts is certainly very commendable if the elevation to the principles of pure reason has already happened and been achieved to complete satisfaction; and that would mean first *founding* the doctrine of morals on metaphysics and, when it has been established, afterwards obtaining *access* for it by means of popularity. But it is without rhyme or reason to want to comply with it in the first investigation, on which all correctness of principles depends. Not only can this procedure never lay claim to the supremely rare merit of a true *philosophical popularity*, since there is no art in making oneself commonly understood when one renounces all thorough insight; it brings to light a disgusting mishmash of gleaned observations and half-rationalizing principles, which dreary pates savor because it is quite useful for everyday chatter, while men of insight feel confused, and discontented – yet unable to help themselves – avert their eyes, even though philosophers, who quite easily see through the dazzling deception, get little hearing when they call for

4:410 suspending this pretended popularity for a while, to earn the rightful permission to be popular only when they have first acquired determinate insight.

One need only look at the essays on morality in that much admired taste, and one will find in a marvelous mixture now the special function of human nature (but once in a while also the idea of a rational nature as such), now perfection, now happiness, here moral feeling, there fear of God, a bit of this and a bit of that; but it does not occur to anyone to ask whether the principles of morality are to be sought in our acquaintance with human nature at all (which after all we can get only from experience) and, if this is not the case – if these principles are to be found completely a priori, free from all that is empirical, simply in pure rational concepts and nowhere else, not even in the least part – to resolve rather to separate off entirely this investigation as pure practical philosophy, or (if one may

---

^f *das Übergewicht*, second edition. The first edition has *die Wahrheit*, which makes no sense. Kant's original manuscript may have read *die Wahl*, "the choice."

employ so notorious a name) as a metaphysics* of morals, to bring it all by itself to its entire completeness, and to put off a public that demands popularity until the conclusion of this undertaking.

But such a completely isolated metaphysics of morals, mixed with no anthropology, no theology, no physics or hyperphysics,^g still less with occult qualities (which one might call hypophysical^h), is not just an indispensable substrate of all theoretical securely determined cognition of duties, but at the same time a desideratum of the highest importance for the actual execution of its prescriptions. For the pure representation of duty, and in general of the moral law, mixed with no alien addition of empirical stimuli, has by the route of reason alone (which in this first becomes aware that by itself it can also be practical) an influence on the human heart so much more powerful than all other incentives[†] one can 4:411 summon from the empirical field, that reason, in the consciousness of its dignity, regards the latter with contempt, and little by little can master them; in the place of which a mixed doctrine of morals, composed of incentives of feelings and inclinations and at the same time of rational concepts, must make the mind waverⁱ between motives that can be brought under no principle, that can lead only very contingently to what is good, but quite often also to what is evil.

It is clear from what has been said that all moral concepts have their seat and origin completely a priori in reason, and indeed in the commonest human reason, just as in that which is speculative in the highest measure;

---

* One can, if one wants to, distinguish (just as pure mathematics is distinguished from applied, and pure logic from applied, thus) pure philosophy of morals (metaphysics) from applied (namely to human nature). Also, by using this label one is reminded at once that moral principles are not to be founded on the peculiarities of human nature but must exist a priori by themselves, and that from such principles it must be possible to derive practical rules for every rational nature, and thus for human nature as well.

† I have a letter from the late excellent *Sulzer*, in which he asks me what the cause may be that the doctrines^j of virtue, however convincing they are to reason, yet accomplish so little.[11] My reply was delayed by my preparations for making it complete. However, it is none other than that the teachers themselves have not purified their concepts, and as they try to do too well by getting hold of motives to moral goodness everywhere, to make their medicine ever so strong, they spoil it. For the commonest observation shows that when one represents an action of righteousness – as it was performed with a steadfast soul, without aiming at any advantage, in this world or another, even under the greatest temptations of need, or of enticement – it leaves far behind and obscures every similar action that was even in the least affected by an alien incentive, that it elevates the soul and stirs up the wish to be able to act like that too. Even children of intermediate age feel this impression, and one should never represent duties to them in any other way.

^g that which lies *beyond* physical nature   ^h that which *underlies* physical nature
ⁱ *schwankend*, second edition; the first has *verwirrt*, "confused"   ^j or "teachings" (of virtue)

that they cannot be abstracted from any empirical and hence merely contingent cognition; that their dignity to serve us as supreme practical principles lies just in this purity of their origin; that every time in adding anything empirical to them one takes away as much from their genuine influence and from the unlimited worth of actions; that it is not only a requirement of the greatest necessity for theoretical purposes, when only speculation counts, but also a matter of the greatest practical importance to draw its concepts and laws from pure reason, to set them forth pure and unmingled, indeed to determine the scope of this entire practical but pure rational cognition, i.e. the entire faculty of pure practical reason, and in so doing not – as speculative philosophy may well permit, indeed at times 4:412 even finds necessary – to make its principles dependent on the particular nature of human reason, but because moral laws are to hold for every rational being as such, already to derive them from the universal concept of a rational being as such, and in this way (as should be possible in this species of entirely separate cognitions) completely to set forth all moral science – which for its *application* to human beings needs anthropology – first independently of this as pure philosophy, i.e. as metaphysics; well aware that without being in its possession it would be futile, I do not say to determine precisely for speculative judging the moral element of duty in everything that conforms with duty, but impossible to found morals on their genuine principles even for the merely common and practical use, principally of moral instruction, and thereby to effect pure moral dispositions and to engraft them on people's minds for the highest good of the world.

However, in order to progress in this work by its natural steps not merely from common moral judging (which is worthy of great respect here) to philosophical, as has been done elsewhere, but from a popular philosophy – that goes no further than it can get by groping by means of examples – to metaphysics (which does not let itself be held back any further by anything empirical and, as it must survey the totality of rational cognition of this kind, perhaps goes up to ideas, where even examples desert us[k]), we must trace and distinctly present the practical rational faculty from its general rules of determination up to where there arises from it the concept of duty.

Every thing in nature works according to laws. Only a rational being has the capacity to act *according to the representation* of laws, i.e. according to principles, or a *will*. Since *reason* is required for deriving actions from laws,

---

[k] The first edition reads "examples that were adequate to the former desert us"

the will is nothing other than practical reason. If reason determines the will without fail, then the actions of such a being that are recognized as objectively necessary are also subjectively necessary; i.e. the will is a capacity to choose *only that* which reason, independently of inclination, recognizes as practically necessary, i.e. as good. If, however, reason all by itself does not sufficiently determine the will, if it is also subject to subjective conditions (to certain incentives) that are not always in agreement with the objective ones; in a word, if the will does not *in itself* completely conform with reason (as is actually the case with human beings), then actions objectively recognized as necessary are subjectively contingent, and the determination of such a will, in conformity with objective laws, is *necessitation*; i.e. the relation of objective laws to a will not altogether good is represented as the determination of the will of a rational being by grounds of reason, to which this will is not, however, according to its nature necessarily obedient. 4:413

The representation of an objective principle in so far as it is necessitating for a will is called a command (of reason), and the formula of the command is called **imperative**.

All imperatives are expressed by an *ought*, and by this indicate the relation of an objective law of reason to a will that according to its subjective constitution is not necessarily determined by it (a necessitation). They say that to do or to omit something would be good, but they say it to a will that does not always do something just because it is represented to it that it would be good to do it. Practically *good*, however, is what determines the will by means of representations of reason, hence not from subjective causes, but objectively, i.e. from grounds that are valid for every rational being, as such. It is distinguished from the *agreeable*, as that which influences the will only by means of sensation from merely subjective causes, which hold only for the senses of this or that one, and not as a principle of reason, which holds for everyone.*

---

* The dependence of the desiderative faculty on sensations is called inclination, and this therefore always proves a *need*. The dependence, however, of a contingently determinable will[1] on principles of reason is called an *interest*. This therefore takes place only within a dependent will, which does not of itself always conform with reason; in the divine will, interest is inconceivable. But even the human will can *take* an *interest* in something without therefore *acting from interest*. The first signifies the *practical* interest in the action, the second the *pathological* interest in the object of the action. The first indicates only dependence of the will on principles of reason by itself, the second on its principles for the sake of inclination, namely when reason states only the practical rule as to how to remedy the need of inclination. In the first case the action interests me, in the second the object of the action (in so far as it is agreeable to me). 4:414 We saw in the first section: that in an action from duty one must pay attention not to the interest in the object, but merely to that in the action itself and in its principle in reason (the law).

[1] second edition; the first edition merely has "of the will"

27

4:414   Thus a perfectly good will would just as much stand under objective laws (of the good), but it could not be represented as thereby *necessitated* to actions that conform with laws, because it can of itself, according to its subjective constitution, be determined only by the representation of the good. Therefore no imperatives hold for the *divine* will and generally for a *holy* will: here the *ought* is out of place, because *willing* already of itself necessarily agrees with the law. Therefore imperatives are only formulae to express the relation of objective laws of willing as such to the subjective imperfection of the will of this or that rational being, e.g. of the human will.

Now, all *imperatives* command either *hypothetically*, or *categorically*. The former represent the practical necessity of a possible action as a means to achieving something else that one wants (or that at least is possible for one to want). The categorical imperative would be the one that represented an action as objectively necessary by itself, without reference to another end.

Because every practical law represents a possible action as good and hence, for a subject practically determinable by reason, as necessary, all imperatives are formulae for the determination of an action necessary according to the principle of a will that is good in some way. Now, if the action would be good merely as a means to *something else*, the imperative is *hypothetical*; if the action is represented as good *in itself*, hence as necessary in a will that in itself conforms to reason, as its principle, then it is *categorical*.

The imperative thus says which action possible by me would be good, and represents the practical rule in relation to a will that does not at once do an action just because it is good, partly because the subject does not always know that it is good, partly because, even if he knew this, his maxims could still be opposed to the objective principles of a practical reason.

The hypothetical imperative thus says only that the action is good for
4:415 some *possible* or *actual* purpose. In the first case it is a **problematically** practical principle, in the second an **assertorically** practical principle. The categorical imperative, which declares the action to be of itself objectively *necessary* without reference to any purpose, i.e. even apart from any other end, holds as an **apodictically** practical principle.

What is possible only by means of powers of some rational being can also be thought as a purpose possible for some will, and therefore there are in fact infinitely many principles of action, in so far as it is represented as necessary for attaining some possible purpose to be effected by it. All sciences have some practical part that consists of tasks to make some end possible for us, and of imperatives as to how it can be attained. These can therefore as such be called imperatives of **skill**. There is no question here whether the end is rational and good, but only what one must do in order to attain it. The prescriptions for the physician thoroughly to cure his man, and for a poisoner reliably to kill him, are of equal worth, in so far as each serves to effect its purpose perfectly. Since in early youth it is unknown what ends we might encounter in life, parents principally seek to have their children learn ever so *many kinds of things*, and take care to develop *skill* in the use of means to all sorts of *discretionary* ends; they cannot determine whether any of them could in the future actually become the purpose of their protégé, while it is entirely *possible* that one day he might have it; and with this they take so much care that they commonly fail to form and to correct their judgment about the worth of the things they might make their ends.

Even so, there is *one* end that can be presupposed as actual in all rational beings (in so far as imperatives suit them, namely as dependent beings), and thus one purpose that they not merely *can* have, but that one can safely presuppose they one and all actually *do have* according to a natural necessity, and that is the purpose of *happiness*. The hypothetical imperative that represents the practical necessity of an action as a means to the advancement of happiness is **assertoric**. One must present it as necessary not merely to some uncertain, merely possible purpose, but to a purpose that one can presuppose safely and a priori^m in every human being, because it belongs to his essence.^n Now, the skill in the choice of 4:416 the means to one's own greatest well-being can be called **prudence*** in the narrowest sense. Thus the imperative that refers to the choice of means to one's own happiness, i.e. the prescription of prudence, is still *hypothetical*; the action is not commanded per se, but just as a means to another purpose.

---

* The word prudence is taken in a twofold sense: in one it may bear the name of worldly prudence, in the other that of private prudence. The first is the skill of a human being to influence others so as to use them for his purposes; the second the insight to unite all these purposes to his own enduring advantage. The latter is actually the one to which even the worth of the former is traced back, and someone who is prudent in the first sense, but not in the second, of him one might better say: he is clever and crafty, and yet on the whole imprudent.

^m "and a priori" was added for the second edition   ^n second edition; the first edition has "nature"

Finally, there is one imperative that – without presupposing as its condition any other purpose to be attained by a certain course of conduct – commands this conduct immediately. This imperative is **categorical**. It concerns not the matter of the action or what is to result from it, but the form and the principle from which it does itself follow; and the essential good in it consists in the disposition, let the result be what it may. This imperative may be called that **of morality**.

Willing according to these three kinds of principles is also clearly distinguished by the *unequal manner* in which they necessitate the will. Now, to make this noticeable they would, I believe, be labeled most suitably in their order by saying that they are either *rules* of skill, or *counsels* of prudence, or *commands* (*laws*) of morality. For only the *law* carries with it the concept of an *unconditional* and indeed objective and hence universally valid *necessity*, and commands are laws that must be obeyed, i.e. must be complied with even contrary to inclination. *Giving counsel* does indeed contain necessity, but it can hold only under a subjective contingent condition, if this or that human being counts this or that as belonging to his happiness; whereas the categorical imperative is limited by no condition, and as absolutely and yet practically necessary can quite properly be called a command. Imperatives of the first kind could also be called *technical* (belonging to art), the second *pragmatic** (to welfare), the third *moral* (belonging to free conduct as such, i.e. to morals).

4:417

Now the question arises: how are all these imperatives possible? This question does not call for knowledge of how to conceive the execution of the action that the imperative commands, but merely of the necessitation of the will that the imperative expresses in its task. How an imperative of skill is possible probably requires no special discussion. Whoever wills the end also wills (in so far as reason has decisive influence on his actions) the indispensably necessary means to it that is in his control. As far as willing is concerned, this proposition is analytic; for in the willing of an object, as my effect, my causality is already thought, as an acting cause, i.e. the use of means, and the imperative already extracts the concept of actions necessary to this end from the concept of a willing of this end (synthetic propositions are certainly needed to determine the means themselves to

---

* Methinks the actual meaning of the word *pragmatic* can be most accurately determined in this way. For *sanctions* are called pragmatic that do not actually flow from the right of states, as necessary laws, but from their *provision* for the general welfare. A *history* is composed in a pragmatic manner if it makes us *prudent*, i.e. instructs the world how it can take care of its advantage better than, or at least just as well as, in previous times.[12]

an intended purpose, but they concern the ground for actualizing not the act of will, but the object). That in order to divide a line into two equal parts according to a reliable principle I must make two intersecting arcs from its extremities, mathematics admittedly teaches by synthetic propositions only; but it is an analytic proposition that – when I know that the effect I have in mind can come about by such action alone – if I completely will the effect I also will the action required for it; for to represent something as an effect possible by me in a certain way, and myself, with regard to it, as acting in this way, that is one and the same thing.

The imperatives of prudence would totally and entirely coincide with those of skill, and be equally analytic, if only it were so easy to provide a determinate concept of happiness. For here as well as there it would be said: whoever wills the end also wills (in conformity with reason necessarily) the only means to it that are in his control. But, unfortunately, the concept of 4:418 happiness is so indeterminate a concept that, even though every human being wishes to achieve it, yet he can never say determinately and in agreement with himself what he actually wishes and wants. The cause of this is: that the elements that belong to the concept of happiness are one and all empirical, i.e. must be borrowed from experience and that, even so, for the idea of happiness an absolute whole is required, a maximum of well-being, in my present and every future condition. Now, it is impossible that the most insightful and at the same time singularly able, but still finite being should make for himself a determinate concept of what he actually wants here. If he wants riches, how much worry, envy and intrigue might he not by this bring down upon his shoulders! If he wants much cognition and insight, that might perhaps only sharpen his eyes all the more, to show him as all the more terrible the ills that are still concealed from him now and yet cannot be avoided, or to burden his desires, which already give him enough trouble, with more needs still. If he wants a long life, who will guarantee him that it would not be a long misery? If at least he wants health, how often has not bodily discomfort kept someone from excess into which unlimited health would have plunged him, and so on. In short, he is not able to determine with complete certainty, according to any principle, what will make him truly happy, because omniscience would be required for this. To be happy, one cannot therefore act on determinate principles, but only according to empirical counsels, e.g. of diet, of thrift, of politeness, of restraint, and so on, which experience teaches on average advance well-being most. From this it follows that the imperatives of prudence cannot, to be precise, command at all, i.e. present actions objectively as practically *necessary*; that they are to be taken rather as counsels (consilia) than as commands (praecepta) of reason; that the problem of determining reliably and universally which action would advance the happiness of a rational being is completely insoluble, and hence that there can be no imperative with regard to it that would in the strict sense command to do what makes us happy because happiness is not an ideal of reason, but of the imagination, which rests merely on empirical grounds, of 4:419 which it is futile to expect that they should determine an action by which the totality of an in fact infinite series of consequences would be attained. This imperative of prudence would, however, be an analytic practical proposition if one assumes that the means to happiness could be reliably stated; for it differs from the imperative of skill only in this, that in the case of the latter the end is merely possible, whereas in the former it is given: but since both merely command the means to that which one presupposes one wills as an end, the imperative that commands willing the means for someone who wills the end is in both cases analytic. There is thus no difficulty with regard to the possibility of such an imperative either.

By contrast, the question of how the imperative of *morality* is possible is no doubt the only one in need of a solution, since it is not hypothetical at all, and thus the objectively represented necessity cannot rely on any presupposition, as in the case of the hypothetical imperatives. However, it is never to slip our attention in this matter that it cannot be made out *by any example*, and hence empirically, whether there is any such imperative at all; but to be dreaded that all imperatives that appear categorical may yet in some hidden way be hypothetical. E.g. when it is said that you ought not to make deceitful promises; and one assumes that the necessity of this omission is not merely giving counsel for avoiding some other ill, so that what is said would be: you ought not to make lying promises lest, if it comes to light, you are deprived of your credit; but that an action° of this kind must be considered as by itself evil, thus that the imperative of the prohibition is categorical; one still cannot establish in any example with certainty that the will is here determined, without another incentive, merely by the law, even if it appears so; for it is always possible that fear of embarrassment, perhaps also an obscure dread of other dangers, may covertly influence the will. Who can prove the non-existence of a cause by experience when all that it teaches is that we do not perceive one? In that

---

° second edition; the first has "but when one asserts that an action"

case, however, the so-called moral imperative, which as such appears categorical and unconditional, would in fact just be a pragmatic prescription that alerts us to our advantage, and merely teaches us to attend to it.

We shall thus have to investigate the possibility of a *categorical* imperative entirely a priori, since we do not here enjoy the advantage that its actuality is being given in experience, in which case its possibility would be necessary not for corroboration, but merely for explanation. For the time being, however, this much can be seen: that the categorical imperative alone expresses a practical **law**, and that the others can indeed one and all be called *principles* of the will, but not laws; since what it is necessary to do merely for attaining a discretionary purpose can be regarded as in itself contingent, and we can always be rid of the prescription if we give up the purpose, whereas the unconditional command leaves the will no free discretion with regard to the opposite, and hence alone carries with it that necessity which we demand for a law. 4:420

Secondly, in the case of this categorical imperative or law of morality the ground of the difficulty (of insight into its possibility) is actually very great. It is an a priori synthetic practical proposition,* and since gaining insight into the possibility of propositions of this kind causes so much difficulty in theoretical cognition, it can easily be inferred that in practical cognition there will be no less.[13]

With this problem, we shall first try to see whether the mere concept of a categorical imperative may perhaps also furnish its formula, which contains the proposition that alone can be a categorical imperative; for how such an absolute command is possible, even if we know how to express it, will still require particular and arduous effort, which we suspend, however, until the final section.

When I think of a *hypothetical* imperative as such I do not know in advance what it will contain, until I am given the condition. But when I think of a *categorical* imperative I know at once what it contains. For since besides the law the imperative contains only the necessity of the maxim† to conform with this law, whereas the law contains no condition to which 4:421

---

* Without a presupposed condition from any inclination, I connect the deed with the will a priori, and hence necessarily (though only objectively, i.e. under the idea of a reason that has complete control over all subjective motives). This is therefore a practical proposition that does not derive the willing of an action analytically from willing another that is already presupposed (for we have no such perfect will), but connects it immediately with the concept of the will of a rational being, as something that is not contained in it.

† A *maxim* is the subjective principle for acting, and must be distinguished from the *objective principle*, namely the practical law. The former contains the practical rule that reason determines in 4:421

it was limited, nothing is left but the universality of a law as such, with which the maxim of the action ought to conform, and it is this conformity alone that the imperative actually represents as necessary.

There is therefore only a single categorical imperative, and it is this: *act only according to that maxim through which you can at the same time will that it become a universal law.*

Now, if from this one imperative all imperatives of duty can be derived as from their principle, then, even though we leave it unsettled whether what is called duty is not as such an empty concept, we shall at least be able to indicate what we think by it and what the concept means.

Since the universality of the law according to which effects happen constitutes that which is actually called *nature* in the most general sense (according to its form), i.e. the existence of things in so far as it is determined according to universal laws, the universal imperative of duty could also be expressed as follows: *so act as if the maxim of your action were to become by your will a* **universal law of nature**.

We shall now enumerate some duties, according to their usual division, into duties to ourselves and to other human beings, into perfect and imperfect duties.*

4:422   1) Someone who feels weary of life because of a series of ills that has grown to the point of hopelessness is still so far in possession of his reason that he can ask himself whether it is not perhaps contrary to a duty to oneself to take one's own life. Now he tries out: whether the maxim of his action could possibly become a universal law of nature. But his maxim is: from self-love I make it my principle to shorten my life if, when pro-tracted any longer, it threatens more ill than it promises agreeableness. The only further question is whether this principle of self-love could become a universal law of nature. But then one soon sees that a nature whose law it were to destroy life itself by means of the same sensation the function of which it is to impel towards the advancement of life, would contradict itself and would thus not subsist as a nature, hence that that

---

conformity with the conditions of the subject (quite often his ignorance, or his inclinations), and is thus the principle according to which the subject *acts*; but the law is the objective principle, valid for every rational being, and the principle according to which it *ought to act*, i.e. an imperative.

* Here one must duly note that I reserve the division of duties entirely for my future *Metaphysics of Morals*, and that this one here is put forward only as discretionary (to order my examples).[14] Further, I here understand by a perfect duty the one that allows of no exception to the advantage of inclination, and then I have not merely external but also internal *perfect duties*, which runs counter to the use of the word adopted in the schools; but I do not mean to answer for it here, since for my purpose it is all one whether or not one concedes it to me.

maxim could not possibly take the place of a universal law of nature, and consequently conflicts entirely with the supreme principle of all duty.

2) Another sees himself pressured by need to borrow money. He knows full well that he will not be able to repay, but also sees that nothing will be lent to him unless he solemnly promises to repay it at a determinate time. He feels like making such a promise; but he still has enough conscience to ask himself: is it not impermissible and contrary to duty to help oneself out of need in such a way? Suppose that he still resolved to do so, his maxim of the action would go as follows: when I believe myself to be in need of money I shall borrow money, and promise to repay it, even though I know that it will never happen. Now this principle of self-love, or of one's own benefit, is perhaps quite consistent with my whole future well-being, but the question now is: whether it is right? I therefore transform the imposition of self-love into a universal law, and arrange the question as follows: how things would stand if my maxim became a universal law. Now, I then see at once that it could never hold as a universal law of nature and harmonize with itself, but must necessarily contradict itself. For the universality of a law that everyone, once he believes himself to be in need, could promise whatever he fancies with the intention not to keep it, would make the promise and the end one may pursue with it itself impossible, as no one would believe he was being promised anything, but would laugh about any such utterance, as a vain pretense.

3) A third finds in himself a talent that by means of some cultivation 4:423 could make him a useful human being in all sorts of respects. However, he sees himself in comfortable circumstances and prefers to give himself up to gratification rather than to make the effort to expand and improve his fortunate natural predispositions. Yet he still asks himself: whether his maxim of neglecting his natural gifts, besides its agreement with his propensity to amusement, also agrees with what one calls duty. Now he sees that a nature could indeed still subsist according to such a universal law, even if human beings (like the South Sea Islanders) should let their talents rust and be intent on devoting their lives merely to idleness, amusement, procreation, in a word, to enjoyment; but he cannot possibly **will** that this become a universal law of nature, or as such be placed in us by natural instinct. For as a rational being he necessarily wills that all capacities in him be developed, because they serve him and are given to him^p for all sorts of possible purposes.

^{p} "and are given to him" is an addition of the second edition

Yet a *fourth*, who is prospering while he sees that others have to struggle with great hardships (whom he could just as well help), thinks: what's it to me? May everyone be as happy as heaven wills, or as he can make himself, I shall take nothing away from him, not even envy him; I just do not feel like contributing anything to his well-being, or his assistance in need! Now, certainly, if such a way of thinking were to become a universal law of nature, the human race could very well subsist, and no doubt still better than when everyone chatters about compassion and benevolence, even develops the zeal to perform such actions occasionally, but also cheats wherever he can, sells out the right of human beings, or infringes it in some other way. But even though it is possible that a universal law of nature could very well subsist according to that maxim, it is still impossible to **will** that such a principle hold everywhere as a law of nature. For a will that resolved upon this would conflict with itself, as many cases can yet come to pass in which one needs the love and compassion of others, and in which, by such a law of nature sprung from his own will, he would rob himself of all hope of the assistance he wishes for himself.

4:424   These, then, are some of the many actual duties, or at least of what we take to be such, whose division^q can clearly be seen from the one principle stated above. One must *be able to will* that a maxim of our action become a universal law: this is as such the canon of judging it morally. Some actions are such that their maxim cannot even be *thought* without contradiction as a universal law of nature; let alone that one could *will* that it *should* become such. In the case of others that inner impossibility is indeed not to be found, but it is still impossible to *will* that their maxim be elevated to the universality of a law of nature, because such a will would contradict itself. It is easy to see that the first conflicts with strict or narrower (unrelenting) duty, the second only with wider (meritorious) duty, and thus that all duties, as far as the kind of obligation (not the object of their action) is concerned, have by these examples been set out completely in their dependence on the one principle.

If we now attend to ourselves in every transgression of a duty, we find that we actually do not will that our maxim should become a universal law, since that is impossible for us, but that its opposite should rather generally

---

^q Both the first and the second original edition have *Abteilung* (division). Editors and translators since the nineteenth century, including Mary Gregor, tend to substitute *Ableitung* ("derivation"), but note that Kant has presented a division of duties that is meant to be evident *from the above principle*, i.e. the fourfold application of the law-of-nature formulation, further explained in the present paragraph.

remain a law; we just take the liberty of making an *exception* to it for ourselves, or[r] (just for this once) to the advantage of our inclination. Consequently, if we considered everything from one and the same point of view, namely that of reason, we would find a contradiction in our own will, namely that a certain principle be objectively necessary as a universal law and yet subjectively should not hold universally, but allow of exceptions. But since we consider our action at one time from the point of view of a will that entirely conforms with reason, but then just the same action also from the point of view of a will affected by inclination, there is actually no contradiction here, but rather a resistance of inclination to the prescription of reason (antagonismus), by which the universality of the principle (universalitas) is transformed into a mere general validity (generalitas), and by this the practical rational principle is meant to meet the maxim halfway. Now, even though this cannot be justified in our own impartially employed judgment, it still proves that we actually acknowledge the validity of the categorical imperative, and permit ourselves (with all respect for it) just a few exceptions that, as it seems to us, are immaterial and wrenched from us.

We have thus established at least this much, that if duty is a concept 4:425 that is to contain significance and actual legislation for our actions it can be expressed only in categorical imperatives, but by no means in hypothetical ones; likewise we have – and this is already a lot – presented distinctly and determined for every use the content of the categorical imperative, which would have to contain the principle of all duty (if there were such a thing at all). But we are not yet ready to prove a priori that such an imperative is actually in place, that there is a practical law, which commands of itself, absolutely and without any incentives, and that following this law is one's duty.

For the purpose of achieving this, it is of the utmost importance to let this serve as a warning, that one must put the thought right out of one's mind that the reality of this principle can be derived from some *particular property of human nature*. For duty is to be practical unconditional necessity of action; it must thus hold for all rational beings (to which an imperative can at all apply), and *only in virtue of this* be a law also for every human will. By contrast, whatever is derived from the special natural predisposition of humanity, from certain feelings and propensity, and

---

[r] It makes good sense to move the bracket to include "or," as Mary Gregor does, to distinguish two kinds of exception: "for oneself" and "for this once," but the change is probably unnecessary.

indeed even, possibly, from a special tendency peculiar to human reason, and would not have to hold necessarily for the will of every rational being – that can indeed yield a maxim for us, but not a law, a subjective principle on which propensity and inclination would fain have us act, but not an objective principle on which we would be *instructed* to act even if every propensity, inclination and natural arrangement of ours were against it; so much so that it proves the sublimity[s] and inner dignity of the command in a duty all the more, the less the subjective causes are in favor of it, and the more they are against it, without thereby weakening in the least the necessitation by the law, or taking anything away from its validity.

Here, then, we in fact see Philosophy placed on a precarious standpoint, which is to be firm even though there is nothing either in heaven, or on earth, from which she is suspended, or on which she relies. Here she is to prove her purity, as the sovereign legislatrix[15] of her laws, not as the herald of those that an implanted sense, or who knows what tutelary nature whispers to her, which yet – though they may still be better than nothing at all – can one and all never make principles that reason dictates, and that must have their source, and with it at the same time their commanding repute, altogether completely a priori: to expect nothing from the inclination of a human being, but everything from the authority of the law and the respect owed to it or, if not, condemn the human being to self-contempt and inner loathing.

4:426

Thus everything that is empirical is not only quite unfit to be added to the principle of morality, it is also most disadvantageous to the purity of morals themselves, in which the actual worth of a will absolutely good and elevated above any price consists precisely in this: that the principle of action is free from all influences of contingent grounds, which only experience can furnish. Against this slackness or even base way of thinking, in seeking to identify the principle from among empirical motives and laws, one cannot actually issue too many or too frequent a warning, as human reason in its weariness gladly rests upon this cushion, and in the dream of sweet pretenses (which instead of Juno let it embrace a cloud)[16] foists on morality a bastard patched up from limbs of quite varied

---

[s] It is impossible to preserve the link between *erhaben* (sublime) and *erhoben* (elevated) in English translation, but readers should bear in mind that *erhaben* means "elevated" to a different, superior rank or sphere.

ancestry, which resembles whatever one wants to see in it, but not Virtue, for him who has once beheld her in her true form.*

The question therefore is this: is it a necessary law *for all rational beings* always to judge their actions according to maxims of which they themselves can will that they serve as universal laws? If it is, then it must (completely a priori) already be bound up with the concept of the will of a rational being as such. But in order to discover this connection one must, however reluctantly, take a step outside, namely into metaphysics, if into a region of it that differs from that of speculative philosophy, namely into the metaphysics of morals. In a practical philosophy, where we are not 4:427 concerned with accepting grounds of what *happens*, but rather laws of what *ought to happen*, even if it never does, i.e. objective practical laws: there we do not need to investigate the grounds of why something pleases or displeases, how the gratification of mere sensation differs from taste, and whether the latter differs from a universal delight of reason; on what feeling pleasure and displeasure rests, and how from this there arise desires and inclinations, and from them, by cooperation of reason, maxims; for all of that belongs to an empirical doctrine of the soul, which would constitute the second part of the doctrine of nature, if considered as *philosophy of nature*, in so far as it is founded on *empirical laws*. But here the objective practical law is at issue, and hence the relation of a will to itself, in so far as it determines itself merely through reason, and then everything that has reference to empirical matters is of itself ruled out; because if *reason all by itself* determines conduct (the possibility of which is just what we now want to investigate), it must necessarily do this a priori.

The will is thought as a capacity to determine itself^t to action *in conformity with the representation of certain laws*. And such a capacity can be found only in rational beings. Now, what serves the will as the objective ground^u of its self-determination is the *end*, and this, if it is given by mere

---

* To behold Virtue in her actual form is nothing other than to present morality stripped of any admixture of the sensuous and any spurious adornment of reward or self-love. Everyone can easily become aware of how much virtue then obscures everything else, that appears enticing to the inclinations, by means of the least effort of his reason if it has not been entirely spoilt for abstraction.

^{t} or "oneself," but the focus on "self-determination" further down makes the translation presented here more likely

^{u} H. J. Paton substitutes "subjective" for "objective"

reason, must hold equally for all rational beings. By contrast, what contains merely the ground of the possibility of an action the effect of which is an end is called the *means*. The subjective ground of desiring is the *incentive*, the objective ground of willing the *motivating ground*; hence the difference between subjective ends, which rest on incentives, and objective ones, which depend on motivating grounds that hold for every rational being. Practical principles are *formal* if they abstract from all subjective ends; they are *material* if they have these, and hence certain incentives, at their foundation. The ends that a rational being intends at its discretion as *effects* of its actions (material ends) are one and all only relative; for merely their relation to a particular kind of desiderative faculty of the subject gives them their worth, which can therefore furnish no universal principles that are valid as well as 4:428 necessary for all rational beings, or for all willing, i.e. practical laws. That is why all these relative ends are the ground of hypothetical imperatives only.

But suppose there were something *the existence of which in itself* has an absolute worth, that, as an *end in itself*, could be a ground of determinate laws, then the ground of a possible categorical imperative, i.e. of a practical law, would lie in it, and only in it alone.

Now I say: a human being and generally every rational being *exists* as an end in itself, *not merely as a means* for the discretionary use for this or that will, but must in all its actions, whether directed towards itself or also to other rational beings, always be considered *at the same time as an end*. All objects of inclinations have a conditional worth only; for if the inclinations, and the needs founded on them, did not exist, their object would be without worth. But the inclinations themselves, as sources of need, are so far from having an absolute worth – so as to make one wish for them as such – that to be entirely free from them must rather be the universal wish of every rational being. Therefore the worth of any object *to be acquired* by our action is always conditional. Beings whose existence rests not indeed on our will but on nature, if they are non-rational beings, still have only a relative worth, as means, and are therefore called *things*, whereas rational beings are called *persons*, because their nature already marks them out as ends in themselves, i.e. as something that may not be used merely as a means, and hence to that extent limits all choice (and is an object of respect). These are therefore not merely subjective ends, the existence of which, as the effect of our action, has a worth *for us*; but rather *objective ends*, i.e. entities[v] whose existence in itself is an end, an end such that no other end can be put in its place, for which they would do service *merely* as means, because without it nothing whatsoever of *absolute worth* could be found; but if all worth were conditional, and hence contingent, then for reason no supreme practical principle could be found at all.

If, then, there is to be a supreme practical principle and, with regard to the human will, a categorical imperative, it must be such that, from the representation of what is necessarily an end for everyone, because it is an *end in itself*, it constitutes an *objective* principle of the will, and hence can 4:429 serve as a universal practical law. The ground of this principle is: *a rational nature[w] exists as an end in itself*. That is how a human being by necessity represents his own existence; to that extent it is thus a *subjective* principle of human actions. But every other rational being also represents its existence in this way, as a consequence of just the same rational ground that also holds for me;* thus it is at the same time an *objective* principle from which, as a supreme practical ground, it must be possible to derive all laws of the will. The practical imperative will thus be the following: *So act that you use humanity, in your own person as well as in the person of any other, always at the same time as an end, never merely as a means.* Let us try to see whether this can be done.

To keep to the previous examples:

First, according to the concept of necessary duty to oneself, someone who is contemplating self-murder[x] will ask himself whether his action can be consistent with the idea of humanity, *as an end in itself*. If to escape from a troublesome condition he destroys himself, he makes use of a person, merely as *a means*, to preserving a bearable condition up to the end of life. But a human being is not a thing, hence not something that can be used *merely* as a means, but must in all his actions always be considered

---

* Here I put this proposition forward as a postulate. The grounds for it will be found in the final section.

[v] In German, there are two words for "thing": *Ding* and *Sache*. *Sache* must be translated "thing" in an ethical context: it is Kant's label for entities that lack freedom and hence moral standing (cf. *Metaphysics of Morals* 6:223). A definition of objective ends as a certain kind of *thing* would therefore be very odd: as moral objects, they are "entities" but not "things" in the moralized sense. However, "thing" is still used to translate the cognate *Ding* elsewhere; *Ding an sich* remains a "thing in itself."

[w] a rational being as such

[x] Kant is availing himself of a morally charged term, of which "self-murder" is the natural and literal translation. This may be significant because, as Gregor notes, in the *Metaphysics of Morals* he hints at possible cases of suicide that might not be morally reprehensible (6:422–424). However, he uses the purely descriptive expression "taking one's life" at 4:422, where the morality of suicide is first discussed.

as an end in itself. Thus the human being in my own person is not at my disposal, so as to maim, to corrupt, or to kill him. (I must here pass over the closer determination of this principle, needed to avoid any misunderstanding, e.g. of amputating limbs to preserve myself, of putting my life in danger to preserve my life, etc.; that belongs to actual moral science.)

Secondly, as far as necessary or owed duty to others is concerned, someone who has it in mind to make a lying promise to others will see at once that he wants to make use of another human being *merely as a means*, who does not at the same time contain in himself the end. For the one I want to use for my purposes by such a promise cannot possibly agree to 4:430 my way of proceeding with him and thus himself contain the end of this action. This conflict with the principle of other human beings can be seen more distinctly if one introduces examples of attacks on the freedom and property of others. For then it is clear that the transgressor of the rights of human beings is disposed to make use of the person of others merely as a means, without taking into consideration that, as rational beings, they are always to be esteemed at the same time as ends, i.e. only as beings who must, of just the same action, also be able to contain in themselves the end.*

Thirdly, with regard to contingent (meritorious) duty to oneself it is not enough that the action not conflict with humanity in our person, as an end in itself, it must also *harmonize with it*. Now there are in humanity predispositions to greater perfection, which belong to the end of nature with regard to humanity in our subject; to neglect these would perhaps be consistent with the *preservation* of humanity, as an end in itself, but not with the *advancement* of this end.

Fourthly, as concerns meritorious duty to others, the natural end that all human beings have is their own happiness. Now, humanity could indeed subsist if no one contributed anything to the happiness of others while not intentionally detracting anything from it; but this is still only a negative and not positive agreement with *humanity, as an end in itself*, if everyone does not also try, as far as he can, to advance the ends of others.

---

* Let it not be thought that the trivial quod tibi non vis fieri etc.ʸ can serve as the benchmark or principle here. For it is, though with various limitations, just derived from the latter; it can be no universal law, for it does not contain the ground of duties to oneself, not of duties of love to others (for many a man would gladly agree that others should not benefit him if only he might be exempt from showing them beneficence), finally not of owed duties to one another; for the criminal would argue on this ground against the judges who punish him, and so on.

ʸ "do not treat others as you would not be treated," a negative formulation of the Golden Rule

For if that representation is to have its *full* effect in me, the ends of a subject that is an end in itself must, as much as possible, also be *my* ends.

This principle of humanity and of every rational nature as such, *as an end in itself* (which is the supreme limiting condition of the freedom of actions 4:431 of every human being) is not borrowed from experience, first, because of its universality, as it aims at all rational beings as such, and about that no experience is sufficient to determine anything; secondly, because in it humanity is represented not as an end of human beings (subjectively), i.e. as an object that by itself one actually makes one's end, but as an objective end that, whatever ends we may have, as a law is to constitute the supreme limiting condition of all subjective ends, and hence must arise from pure reason. For the ground of all practical legislation lies *objectively in the rule* and the form of universality, which (according to the first principle) makes it capable of being a law (or perhaps a law of nature), *subjectively*, however, *in the end*; the subject of all ends, however, is every rational being, as an end in itself (according to the second principle): from this now follows the third practical principle of the will, as the supreme condition of its harmony with universal practical reason, the idea *of the will of every rational being as a universally legislating will.*[z]

According to this principle, all maxims are rejected that are not consistent with the will's own universal legislation. Thus the will is not just subject to the law, but subject in such a way that it must also be viewed *as self-legislating*,[a] and just on account of this as subject to the law (of which it can consider itself the author[b]) in the first place.

The imperatives according to the previous mode of representation – namely of actions in conformity with law generally similar to a *natural order*, or of the universal *precedence of the end*[c] of rational beings in

---

[z] *eines allgemein gesetzgebenden Willens.* Here, and in the sequel, a more literal translation replaces Gregor's "a will giving universal laws." As to "lawgiving" vs. "legislation," Gregor is right that "legislation" and "legislator" naturally refer to the sphere of positive law, which Kant did not have in mind in the *Groundwork*; but then, so do *Gesetzgebung* and *Gesetzgeber* in German. Kant is clearly availing himself of a political metaphor.

[a] More literal than Gregor's "as giving the law to itself," and again preferable. As she notes, *selbstgesetzgebend* might be taken to refer to legislation *by* the self as well as legislation *to* the self. In her translation, the former is implied but the emphasis clearly rests on the latter. However, Kant's argument in general, and at 4:440 in particular, would seem to emphasize the former. What is important is that the will must be viewed *as itself legislating*. The present translation preserves the ambiguity and thus leaves the interpretative question open.

[b] in the sense of "originator"

[c] *Zwecksvorzuges*, a tricky word, which Kant uses only once, at this point in the *Groundwork*; human beings as ends take universal precedence in the order of ends, and the ends of human beings deserve universal preferential treatment.

themselves – did exclude from their commanding repute any admixture of interest, as an incentive, precisely because they were represented as categorical; but they were only *assumed* to be categorical because such an assumption was necessary if one wanted to explicate the concept of duty. But that there are practical propositions that command categorically could not of itself be proved, just as little as this can generally be done at present, in this section; one thing, however, could yet have been done, namely: that the dissociation from all interest in willing from duty, as the specific mark distinguishing categorical from hypothetical imperatives, be indicated in

4:432 the imperative itself, by means of some determination that it contains, and this is done in the present third formula of the principle, namely the idea of the will of every rational being, as a *universally legislating will*.

For when we think of such a will, then, even though a will *that stands under laws* may still be bound to this law by means of some interest, yet a will that is itself the supreme legislator cannot possibly, as such, depend on any interest; for such a dependent will would itself require yet another law to limit the interest of its self-love to the condition of a validity to be a universal law.

Thus the *principle* of every human will as *a will universally legislating through all its maxims*,* if it is otherwise correct, would be very *well fitted* to be the categorical imperative, in that, precisely for the sake of the idea of universal legislation, it *is founded on no interest* and can thus alone, among all possible imperatives, be *unconditional*; or better still, by converting the proposition, if there is a categorical imperative (i.e. a law for every will of a rational being), then it can only command to do everything from the maxim of one's will as one that could at the same time have as its object itself as universally legislating; for only then is the practical principle, and the imperative the will obeys, unconditional, because it can have no interest whatsoever at its foundation.

Now, if we look back on all the efforts that have ever been undertaken to detect the principle of morality to this day, it is no wonder why one and all they had to fail. One saw the human being bound to laws by his duty, but it did not occur to anyone that he is subject *only to his own* and yet *universal legislation*, and that he is only obligated to act in conformity with his own will which is, however, universally legislating according to its

---

* I can be exempted from citing examples to illustrate this principle, since those that first illustrated the categorical imperative and its formula can all serve just that purpose here.

natural end.[d] For if one thought of him just as subject to a law (whichever it may be), it had to carry with it some interest as stimulation or constraint, 4:433 because it did not as a law arise from *his* will, which instead was necessitated by *something else*, in conformity with a law, to act in a certain way. Because of this entirely necessary conclusion, however, all the labor of finding a supreme ground of duty was irretrievably lost. For one never got duty, but the necessity of an action from a certain interest, be it one's own interest or that of another. But then the imperative always had to be conditional, and could not be fit to be a moral command at all. I shall therefore call this principle the principle[e] of the **autonomy** of the will, in opposition to every other, which I accordingly count as **heteronomy**.

The concept of every rational being that must consider itself as universally legislating through all the maxims of its will, so as to judge itself and its actions from this point of view, leads to a very fruitful concept attached to it, namely that *of a kingdom[f] of ends.*

By a *kingdom*, however, I understand the systematic union of several rational beings through common laws.[g] Now, since laws determine ends according to their universal validity, it is possible – if one abstracts from the personal differences among rational beings, and likewise from all content of their private ends – to conceive a whole of all ends (of rational beings as ends in themselves, as well as the ends of its own that each of them may set for itself) in systematic connection, i.e. a kingdom of ends, which is possible according to the above principles.

For all rational beings stand under the *law* that each of them is to treat itself and all others *never merely as a means*, but always *at the same time as an end in itself*. But by this there arises a systematic union of rational beings through common objective laws, i.e. a kingdom, which – because what these laws have as their purpose is precisely the reference of these beings to one another, as ends and means – can be called a kingdom of ends (of course only an ideal).

A rational being, however, belongs to the kingdom of ends as a *member* if it is universally legislating in it, but also itself subject to these laws. It belongs to it *as its head* if as legislating it is not subject to the will of another.

[d] *dem Naturzwecke nach*
[e] *diesen Grundsatz das Prinzip*, second edition; the first edition has merely "this principle" (*dieses Prinzip*), which does not make sense
[f] or "realm," "commonwealth"   [g] in the sense of "communal" or "shared"

4:434   A rational being must always consider itself as legislating in a kingdom of ends possible through freedom of the will, whether as a member, or as its head. It cannot, however, occupy the position of the latter merely by the maxims of its will, but only if it is a completely independent being, without need or limitation of its capacities adequate to the will.

Morality thus consists in referring all action to the legislation by which alone a kingdom of ends is possible. This legislation must, however, be found in every rational being itself, and be able to arise from its will, the principle of which is thus: to do no action on a maxim other than in such a way, that it would be consistent with it that it be a universal law, and thus only in such a way *that the will could through its maxim consider itself as at the same time universally legislating*. Now, if maxims are not already by their nature in agreement with this objective principle of rational beings, as universally legislating, the necessity of an action according to this principle is called practical necessitation, i.e. *duty*. Duty does not apply to the head in the kingdom of ends, but it does to every member of it, and indeed to all in equal measure.

The practical necessity of acting according to this principle, i.e. duty, does not at all rest on feelings, impulses, or inclinations, but merely on the relation of rational beings to one another, in which the will of a rational being must always at the same time be considered as *legislating*, since it could not otherwise be thought as an *end in itself*. Reason thus refers every maxim of the will as universally legislating to every other will, and also to every action towards oneself, and it does so not for the sake of any other practical motivating ground or future advantage, but from the idea of the *dignity* of a rational being that obeys no law other than that which at the same time it itself gives.

In the kingdom of ends everything has either a **price**, or a **dignity**. What has a price can be replaced with something else, as its *equivalent*; whereas what is elevated above any price, and hence allows of no equivalent, has a dignity.

What refers to general human inclinations and needs has a *market price*; what, even without presupposing a need, conforms with a certain taste,
4:435 i.e. a delight in the mere purposeless play of the powers of our mind, has a *fancy price*; but what constitutes the condition under which alone something can be an end in itself does not merely have a relative worth, i.e. a price, but an inner worth, i.e. *dignity*.

Now, morality is the condition under which alone a rational being can be an end in itself; because it is possible only by this to be a legislating member in the kingdom of ends. Thus morality and humanity, in so far as it is capable of morality, is that which alone has dignity. Skill and diligence in work have a market price; wit, lively imagination, and humor have a fancy price; by contrast, fidelity in promising and benevolence from principles (not from instinct) have an inner worth. If these are lacking, neither nature nor art contains anything that they could put in their place; for their worth does not consist in the effects that arise from them, in the advantage and utility they provide, but in the dispositions – i.e. the maxims of the will – which in this way readily reveal themselves in actions, even if the result were not to favor them. Also, these actions need no recommendation from any subjective proclivity[h] or taste to look upon them with immediate favor and delight, from any immediate propensity or feeling for them; they represent the will that performs them as the object of an immediate respect, for which nothing but reason is required to *impose* them upon the will, not to *coax* them out of it, which latter would be a contradiction in the case of duties anyway. This estimation thus lets us recognize the worth of such a way of thinking as dignity, and puts it infinitely above any price, with which it cannot be balanced or compared at all without, as it were, violating its sanctity.

And what is it, then, that entitles a morally good disposition or virtue to make such high claims? It is nothing less than the *share* it obtains for a rational being *in universal legislation*, by which it makes it fit to be a member of a possible kingdom of ends, which it was already destined to be by its own nature, as an end in itself and precisely in virtue of this as legislating in the kingdom of ends, as free with regard to all laws of nature, obeying only those that it itself gives and according to which its maxims can belong to a universal legislation (to which he[i] at the same time subjects himself). For nothing has any worth other than that which the law determines for it. But precisely because of this, the legislation that determines all worth must itself have a dignity, i.e. unconditional, incomparable worth, for which the word *respect* alone makes a befitting

4:436

---

[h] *Disposition*; to be distinguished from an agent's *Gesinnung* ("disposition"), a term used above and there equated with an agent's maxims, i.e. subjective principles of action. For Kant, a *disposition* is a habitual proclivity to act in a certain way, as distinguished from one's (natural) temperament, see *Anthropology* 7:286.13.

[i] Kant slips back into using the masculine pronoun associated with "human being" (*der Mensch*) rather than the neuter of "being" (*das Wesen*). This is not uncommon. There is no need to change the text.

expression of the estimation a rational being is to give of it. *Autonomy* is thus the ground of the dignity of a human and of every rational nature.

The above three ways of representing the principle of morality are fundamentally only so many formulae of the selfsame law, one of which[j] of itself unites the other two within it. However, there is yet a dissimilarity among them, which is indeed subjectively rather than objectively practical, namely to bring an idea of reason closer to intuition (according to a certain analogy) and thereby to feeling. For all maxims have

1) a *form*, which consists in universality, and then the formula of the moral imperative is expressed as follows: that maxims must be chosen as if they were to hold as universal laws of nature;

2) a *matter*, namely an end, and then the formula says: that a rational being, as an end according to its nature, and hence as an end in itself, must serve for every maxim as the limiting condition of all merely relative and arbitrary ends;

3) a *complete determination* of all maxims by that formula, namely: that all maxims from one's own legislation ought to harmonize into a possible kingdom of ends as a kingdom of nature.* Here the progression takes place as through the categories of the *unity* of the form of the will (its universality), the *plurality* of the matter (of objects, i.e. of ends), and the *allness* or totality of the system of these. But in moral *judging* it is better always to proceed by the strict method, and make the foundation the universal formula[k] of the categorical imperative: *act according to the maxim*
4:437 *that can make itself at the same time a universal law.* If, however, one wants at the same time to obtain *access* for the moral law, it is very useful to lead one and the same action through the said three concepts and thereby, as far as can be done, bring it closer to intuition.

We can now end where we set out from at the beginning, namely with the concept of an unconditionally good will. A *will is absolutely good* that cannot be evil, hence whose maxim, if made a universal law, can never conflict with itself. This principle is therefore also its supreme law: act

---

* Teleology considers nature as a kingdom of ends, moral science a possible kingdom of ends as a kingdom of nature. There the kingdom of ends is a theoretical idea for explaining what exists. Here it is a practical idea for the sake of bringing about – in conformity with precisely this idea – what does not exist but can become actual by means of our behavior.

[j] Gregor, among others, translates the text to the effect that *each* of the three formulae must contain the other two within itself, but that is not what Kant is saying. *One* of the variants (the third of the formulations mentioned here) contains within it the other two (the first and the second).

[k] or perhaps "general formula"

always on that maxim the universality of which as a law you can will at the same time; this is the only condition under which a will can never be in conflict with itself, and such an imperative is categorical. Since the validity of the will, as a universal law for possible actions, has an analogy with the universal connection of the existence of things according to universal laws, which is what is formal in nature as such, the categorical imperative can also be expressed as follows: *act according to maxims that can at the same time have as their object themselves as universal laws of nature.* Such, then, is the formula of an absolutely good will.

A rational nature is distinguished from the others by this, that it sets itself an end. This end would be the matter of every good will. But since, in the idea of a will absolutely good without any limiting condition (of attaining this or that end) one must abstract altogether from every end to be *effected* (which would make every will only relatively good), the end must here be thought not as an end to be effected *but as an independently existing* end, and hence only negatively, i.e. that which must never be contravened in action, and which must therefore be esteemed in every willing never merely as a means, but always at the same time as an end. Now, this end can be nothing other than the subject of all possible ends itself because it is also the subject of a possible absolutely good will; for it cannot, without contradiction, be ranked lower than any other object. Accordingly, the principle: so act with reference to every rational being (to yourself and others) that in your maxim it counts at the same time as an end in itself, is fundamentally one and the same as the principle: act on a maxim that at the same time contains in itself its own universal validity 4:438 for every rational being. For to say that in the use of means to any end I ought to limit my maxim to the condition of its universal validity, as a law for every subject, is tantamount to saying that the subject of ends, i.e. the rational being itself, must be made the foundation of all maxims of actions, never merely as a means, but as the supreme limiting condition in the use of all means, i.e. always at the same time as an end.

Now, from this follows indisputably: that every rational being, as an end in itself, must be able to view itself as at the same time universally legislating with regard to any law whatsoever to which it may be subject, because it is just this fittingness of its maxims for universal legislation that marks it out as an end in itself; likewise that this dignity (prerogative) it has above all merely natural beings brings with it that it must always take its maxims from the point of view of itself, but also at the same time of every other rational being as legislating (which are therefore also called persons). Now in this way a world of rational beings (mundus intelligibilis[l]) as a kingdom of ends is possible, and possible through their own legislation of all persons as members. Accordingly, every rational being must so act as if through its maxims it were at all times a legislating member of the universal kingdom of ends. The formal principle of these maxims is: so act as if your maxim were to serve at the same time as a universal law (of all rational beings). Thus a kingdom of ends is possible only according to the analogy with a kingdom of nature – but the former just according to maxims, i.e. self-imposed rules, the latter just according to laws of externally necessitated efficient causes. Regardless of this, the whole of nature, even though it is viewed as a machine, is still – in so far as it has reference to rational beings as its ends – given for that reason the name of a kingdom of nature. Now, such a kingdom of ends would actually come about through maxims the rule of which the categorical imperative prescribes to all rational beings *if they were universally followed*. But even though a rational being that itself were to follow this maxim punctiliously cannot, because of that, count on every other to be true to it as well, or likewise that the kingdom of nature and its purposive order harmonize with him, as a fitting member, into a kingdom of ends possible through himself,[m] i.e. that his expectation of happiness be favored; nevertheless that law: act according to the maxims of a member universally legislating for a merely possible kingdom of ends, remains in its full force because it commands categorically. And the paradox lies just in this: that the mere dignity of humanity, as rational nature, without any other end or advantage to be attained by it, and hence respect for a mere idea, is still to serve as an unrelenting prescription of the will, and that it is just in this independence of a maxim from all such incentives that its sublimity consists, and the worthiness of every rational subject to be a legislating member in the kingdom of ends; for otherwise he would have to be represented only as subject to the natural law of his needs. Even if the natural kingdom as well as the kingdom of ends were thought as united under one head, and by this the latter would no longer remain a mere idea but obtain true reality, it would thereby no doubt gain the supplement of a strong incentive, but never any increase in its inner worth; for regardless of this, even this sole limitless legislator would still

4:439

---

[l] intelligible world   [m] Kant once again slips back into using the masculine form.

have to be represented as judging the worth of rational beings only by their disinterested conduct, prescribed to them directly, merely from that idea. The essence of things is not altered by their external relations; and it is according to what alone – without thinking of the latter – constitutes the worth of a human being that he must also be judged by anyone whatsoever, even by the supreme being. *Morality* is thus the relation of actions to the autonomy of the will, that is, to the possible universal legislation through its maxims. An action that can be consistent with the autonomy of the will is *permissible;* one that does not agree with it is *impermissible.* A will whose maxims necessarily harmonize with the laws of autonomy is a *holy*, absolutely good will. The dependence on the principle of autonomy of a will that is not absolutely good (moral necessitation) is *obligation.* This cannot therefore refer to a holy being. The objective necessity of an action from obligation is called *duty.*

From what has just been said it is now easy to explain how it can be: that, although we think of the concept of duty in terms of subjection to the law, yet at the same time we thereby picture a certain sublimity and *dignity* 4:440 in the person who fulfills all his duties. For there is indeed no sublimity in him in so far as he is *subject* to the moral law; but there is, in so far as with regard to it he is at the same time *legislating* and only because of that subordinated to it. Also, we have shown above how neither fear, nor inclination, but solely respect for the law is the incentive that can give an action a moral worth. Our own will, in so far as it would act only under the condition of a possible universal legislation through its maxims – this will possible for us in the idea – is the actual object of respect, and the dignity of humanity consists in just this capability, to be universally legislating, if with the proviso of also being itself subject to precisely this legislation.

The autonomy of the will as the supreme principle of morality

Autonomy of the will is the characteristic of the will by which it is a law to itself (independently of any characteristic of the objects of willing). The principle of autonomy is thus: not to choose in any other way than that the maxims of one's choice are also comprised as universal law in the same willing. That this practical rule is an imperative, i.e. that the will of every rational being is necessarily bound to it as a condition, cannot be proved by mere analysis of the concepts that occur in it, because it is a synthetic proposition; one would have to go beyond the cognition of objects to a critique of the subject, i.e. of pure practical reason, since this synthetic proposition, which commands apodictically, must be capable of being cognized completely a priori; this business, however, does not belong in the present section. But that the envisaged principle of autonomy is the sole principle of moral science can very well be established by mere analysis of the concepts of morality. For thereby we find that its principle must be a categorical imperative, and that it commands neither more nor less than just this autonomy.

4:441

The heteronomy of the will as the source of all spurious principles of morality

If it is *in anything other* than the fitness of its maxims for its own universal legislation, hence if – as it goes beyond itself – it is in a characteristic of any of its objects that the will seeks the law that is to determine it, the outcome is always *heteronomy*. Then the will does not give itself the law, but the object by its relation to the will gives the law to it. This relation, whether it rests on inclination, or on representations of reason, makes possible hypothetical imperatives only: I ought to do something *because I want something else*. By contrast, the moral and hence categorical imperative says: I ought to act in such or such a way, even if I did not want anything else. E.g. the former says: I ought not to lie if I want to maintain my honorable reputation; but the latter: I ought not to lie even if it did not bring on me the least disgrace. The latter must therefore abstract from all objects to this extent, that they have no *influence* whatsoever on the will, so that practical reason (the will) may not merely administer alien interest, but merely prove its own commanding repute, as supreme legislation. Thus I ought e.g. to try to advance the happiness of others, not as if its existence made any difference to me (whether because of immediate inclination, or some delight indirectly through reason), but merely because the maxim that excludes it cannot be comprised in one and the same willing, as universal law.

Division of all possible principles of morality from the assumed fundamental concept of heteronomy

Here, as everywhere in its pure use, human reason has, as long as it lacks critique, first tried every possible wrong route before successfully hitting on the only true one.

All principles that can be entertained from this point of view are either *empirical* or *rational*. The **first**, from the principle of *happiness*, are built on physical or moral feeling; the **second**, from the principle of *perfection*, either on that rational concept, as a possible effect of our will, or on the concept of an independently existing perfection (the will of God), as its determining cause.

Empirical principles are not fit to be the foundation of moral laws at all. For the universality with which they are to hold for all rational beings regardless of differences – the unconditional practical necessity that is thereby imposed upon them – vanishes if their ground is taken from the *particular arrangement of human nature*, or the contingent circumstances in which it is placed. Yet the principle of *one's own happiness*[17] is the most objectionable, not merely because it is false, and experience contradicts the pretense that being well always tallies with behaving well, nor merely because it contributes nothing whatsoever to the grounding of morality, as making a human being happy is something entirely different from making him good, and making him prudent and wise in matters of his own advantage from making him virtuous: but because it underpins morality with incentives that rather undermine it and annihilate all its sublimity, since they put motives to virtue and those to vice in the same class and only teach us to improve our calculations, but quench totally and entirely the specific difference between the two; whereas moral feeling – this supposed special sense* (however shallow appealing to it is, as those who cannot *think* believe they can, even where merely universal laws count, help themselves out by *feeling*, even though feelings, which by nature differ infinitely in degree from one another, can do little to yield a uniform measure of good and evil, and one by his feeling cannot validly judge for others at all) – still remains closer to morality and its dignity because it does Virtue the honor of attributing to her *immediately* the delight and high esteem we have for her, and does not, as it were, tell her to her face that it is not her beauty, but only our advantage that ties us to her.

Among the *rational* or reason-based grounds of morality, the ontological concept of *perfection*[19] (however empty, however indeterminate, and

4:442

4:443

---

* I class the principle of moral feeling with that of happiness because every empirical interest promises to contribute to our well-being by the agreeableness that something has to offer, whether this happens immediately and without a view to advantages, or with regard for them. Likewise one must, with *Hutcheson*, class the principle of compassion for the happiness of others with that moral sense assumed by him.[18]

hence useless it may be for finding, in the immense field of possible reality, the greatest sum fitting for us, and however much, in trying specifically to distinguish the reality that is here in question from every other, it has an unavoidable propensity to revolve around in a circle, and covertly to presuppose the morality it is supposed to explain) is still better than the theological concept,[20] of deriving morality from a divine all-perfect will, not merely because we cannot intuit its perfection but can derive it from our concepts alone, the foremost of which is that of morality, but because if we do not do this (as it would, if we did, be a crude explanatory circle), the concept of His will still left to us – taken from the attributes of desire for honor and dominion, combined with horrendous representations of power and the zeal for vengeance – would have to be the foundation for a system of morals directly opposed to morality.

But if I had to choose between the concept of a moral sense and that of perfection as such (both of which at least do not infringe on morality, even though they are quite unfit to support it as its foundation): then I would settle for the latter; because – since at least it removes the decision of the question from sensibility to the judicial court of pure reason – even if it decides nothing here, it still preserves unaltered the indeterminate idea (of a will good in itself) for closer determination.

Further, I believe I may be exempt from a lengthy refutation of all these doctrinal systems. It is so easy, and presumably so well understood even by those whose office requires them to declare themselves for one of these theories (because their audience will not suffer suspension of judgment), that it would only be superfluous labor. But what here interests us more, is to know: that these principles set up nothing other than heteronomy of the will as the first ground of morality, and precisely because of this must necessarily miss their mark.

4:444 Wherever an object of the will has to be made the foundation for prescribing the rule that determines it, there the rule is nothing other than heteronomy; the imperative is conditional, namely: *if* or *because* one wills this object, one ought to act in such or such a way; hence it can never command morally, i.e. categorically. Whether the object determines the will by means of inclination, as with the principle of one's own happiness, or by means of reason directed to objects of our possible willing as such, in the case of the principle of perfection, the will never determines itself *immediately*, by the representation of the action, but only by an incentive that the anticipated effect of the action has on the will: *I ought*

54

to do something because I want something else, and here yet another law must
be made the foundation in my subject, according to which I necessarily will
this something else, and this law in turn requires an imperative to limit this
maxim. For because the impulse that the representation of an object
possible through our powers is to exert on the will of the subject, according
to his natural constitution, belongs to the nature of the subject – whether to
sensibility (to inclination and taste) or to understanding and reason, which
by the special arrangement of their nature take delight in being exercised
on an object – it would[n] actually be nature that gives the law, which, as
such, must not only be cognized and proved by experience, and hence is in
itself contingent and unfit to be an apodictic practical rule, such as the
moral one must be, but it is *always only heteronomy* of the will: the will does
not give the law to itself, but an alien impulse gives it to it, by means of a
nature of the subject that is attuned to its receptivity.

An absolutely good will, whose principle must be a categorical imperative, will therefore, indeterminate with regard to all objects, contain
merely the *form of willing* as such, and indeed as autonomy; i.e. the fitness
of the maxim of every good will to make itself into a universal law is itself
the sole law that the will of every rational being imposes upon itself,
without underpinning it with any incentive or interest as its foundation.

How such a synthetic practical proposition a priori is possible and why it is
necessary, is a problem that cannot be resolved within the bounds of the
metaphysics of morals, nor have we asserted its truth here, much less 4:445
pretended that it is within our control to give a proof. By unraveling the
concept of morality generally in vogue, we showed only: that an autonomy
of the will unavoidably attaches to it, or rather lies at its foundation.
Whoever takes morality to be something, and not a chimerical idea without truth, must therefore also concede its principle stated above. This
section, just like the first, was thus merely analytic. Now, that morality is
no phantasm – which follows if the categorical imperative and with it the
autonomy of the will is true, and absolutely necessary as an a priori
principle – requires a *possible synthetic use of pure practical reason*, which
we cannot, however, venture upon without a prior *critique* of this rational
faculty itself, the principal features of which, as sufficient for our purpose,
we shall have to present in the final section.

---

[n] second edition; the problematic text of the first edition reads: "reason takes in perfection as such
(the existence of which depends either on itself, or only on the highest independently existing
perfection), it would"

Third section

Transition from the metaphysics of morals to the critique of pure practical reason

The concept of freedom is the key to the explanation of the autonomy of the will

A *will* is a kind of causality of living beings in so far as they are rational, and *freedom* would be that property of such a causality, as it can be efficient independently of alien causes *determining* it; just as *natural necessity* is the property of the causality of all non-rational beings to be determined to activity by the influence of alien causes.

The explication of freedom stated above is *negative* and therefore unfruitful for gaining insight into its essence; but there flows from it a *positive* concept of freedom, which is so much the richer and more fruitful. Since the concept of causality carries with it that of *laws* according to which, by something that we call a cause, something else, namely the consequence, must be posited: freedom, though it is not a property of the will according to natural laws, is not lawless because of that at all, but must rather be a causality according to immutable laws, but of a special kind; for otherwise a free will would be an absurdity. Natural necessity was a heteronomy of efficient causes; for every effect was possible only according to the law that something else determines the efficient cause to causality; what else, then, can freedom of the will be, but autonomy, i.e. the property of the will of being a law to itself? But the proposition: the will is in all actions a law to itself, designates only the principle of acting on no maxim other than that which can also have itself as its object as a universal law. But this is just the formula of the categorical imperative and the principle of morality: thus a free will and a will under moral laws are one and the same.

Thus if freedom of the will is presupposed, morality along with its principle follows from it, by mere analysis of its concept. Yet the latter is always a synthetic proposition: an absolutely good will is that whose maxim can always contain itself, considered as a universal law; for by analysis of the concept of a will good per se, that property of its maxim cannot be found. Such synthetic propositions are possible only by this, that both cognitions are bound together by their connection with a third thing in which they are both to be found. The *positive* concept of freedom provides this third thing, which cannot, as in the case of physical causes, be the nature of the world of sense (in the concept of which the concepts of something as the cause, in relation to *something else* as the effect, come together). What this third thing is, to which freedom points us, and of which we a priori have an idea, cannot yet at once be indicated here – and make comprehensible the deduction of the concept of freedom from pure practical reason, and with it the possibility of a categorical imperative – but still requires some preparation.

Freedom must be presupposed as a property of the will of all rational beings

It is not enough that, on whatever grounds, we attribute freedom to our will if we do not have grounds sufficient to attribute it to all rational beings as well. For since morality serves as a law for us only as for *rational beings*, it must hold for all rational beings as well, and as it must be derived solely from the property of freedom, freedom must also be proved as a property of the will of all rational beings; and it is not enough to establish it from certain supposed experiences of human nature (though this is actually absolutely impossible and can solely be established a priori), but one must prove it as belonging to the activity of rational beings endowed with a will as such. Now I say: every being that cannot act otherwise than *under the idea of freedom* is actually free, in a practical respect, precisely because of that; i.e. all laws that are inseparably bound up with freedom hold for it just as if its will had also been declared free in itself, and in a way that is valid in theoretical philosophy.* Now I assert: that we must necessarily

4:448

---

* I follow this route – of assuming freedom only, sufficient for our purpose, as made the foundation by human beings in their actions merely *in the idea* – so that I may not incur the obligation of proving freedom in its theoretical respect as well. For even if this latter point is left unsettled, the

lend to every rational being that has a will also the idea of freedom, under which alone it acts. For in such a being we conceive a reason that is practical, i.e. has causality with regard to its objects. Now, one cannot possibly think of a reason that would self-consciously receive guidance° from any other quarter with regard to its judgments, since the subject would not then attribute the determination of judgment to his reason, but to an impulse. Reason must view herself as the authoress^P of her principles, independently of alien influences, and must consequently, as practical reason, or as the will of a rational being, by herself be viewed as free; i.e. its will can be a will of its own only under the idea of freedom, and must thus for practical purposes be ascribed to all rational beings.

Of the interest that attaches to the ideas of morality

We last traced the determinate concept of morality back to the idea of freedom; which we could not, however, prove as something actual even in 4:449 ourselves or in human nature; we saw only that we must presuppose it if we want to think of a being as rational and endowed with consciousness of its causality with regard to its actions, i.e. with a will; and thus we find that on just the same grounds we must ascribe this property of determining itself to action under the idea of its freedom to every being endowed with reason and will.

But there also flowed from the presupposition of these ideas the consciousness of a law for acting: that the subjective principles of actions, i.e. maxims, must always be so taken that they can also hold objectively, i.e. universally as principles, and hence serve for our own universal legislation. But why, then, ought I to subject myself to this principle, and do so as a rational being as such, and hence thereby also all other beings endowed with reason? I am willing to concede that no interest *impels* me to do this, for that would yield no categorical imperative; but I must still necessarily *take* an interest in it, and see how this can be; for this ought is actually a willing that holds for every rational being, on the condition: if reason were practical in it without hindrances;

---

same laws that would bind a being that was actually free yet hold for a being that cannot act otherwise than under the idea of its own freedom. Here we can thus liberate ourselves from the burden that weighs upon theory.

° or "be steered." *Lenkung* suggests an external power in charge of the activities of reason
^P As elsewhere, Kant is clearly using personification as a stylistic device in this passage, which is why an attempt has been made to reproduce the allegorical style of the original.

but for beings who, like us, are also affected by sensibility, as incentives of a different kind, and in whose case what reason all by itself would do is not always done, that necessity of action is only called an ought, and the subjective necessity is distinguished from the objective one.

Thus it seems as if in the idea of freedom we actually just presupposed the moral law, namely the principle of the autonomy of the will itself, and could not by itself prove its reality and objective necessity; and then we should still have gained something quite considerable, because we would at least have determined the genuine principle more accurately than was perhaps done elsewhere, but with regard to its validity, and the practical necessity of subjecting oneself to it, we would have got no further; for if someone were to ask us why the universal validity of our maxim, as a law, must be the limiting condition of our actions, and on what we found the worth we assign to this way of acting, which is to be so great that there can be no higher interest at all, and how it can be that a human being believes that he feels his personal worth in virtue of this alone, compared to which 4:450 that of an agreeable or disagreeable condition should be taken for nothing, we would not be able to give him a satisfactory answer.

We do indeed find that we can take an interest in a personal characteristic that carries with it no interest whatsoever in a condition, if only the former makes us capable of partaking of the latter, in case reason were to effect its distribution, i.e. that the mere worthiness to be happy, even without the motivating ground of partaking of this happiness, can interest of itself: but this judgment is in fact only the effect of already presupposing the importance of moral laws (when by the idea of freedom we detach ourselves from all empirical interest); but we cannot yet come to see in this way that we ought to detach ourselves from it – i.e. consider ourselves as free in acting, and thus still take ourselves to be subject to certain laws, so as to find merely in our own person a worth that can make good to us the loss of everything that obtains a worth for our condition – or how this is possible, and hence *whence the moral law is binding.*[q]

There appears at this point, one must freely admit it, a kind of circle from which, as it seems, there is no escape. We take ourselves to be free in the order of efficient causes so as to think ourselves under moral laws in the order of ends, and we afterwards think ourselves as subject to these laws because we have ascribed to ourselves freedom of the will; for

---

[q] or "obligates," i.e. the ground or source of obligation remains obscure

freedom and the will's own legislation are both autonomy, and hence reciprocal concepts; but precisely because of this one of them cannot be used to explicate the other or to state its ground, but at most only to reduce to a single concept, for logical purposes, representations of just the same object that appear dissimilar (as different fractions of equal value are reduced to their lowest terms).

Yet there still remains for us one way out, namely to try: whether when, through freedom, we think of ourselves as causes efficient a priori we do not take up a standpoint that is different from when we represent ourselves according to our actions as effects that we see before our eyes.

It is an observation for which no subtle thinking is required, but one that one may assume the commonest understanding can make, though 4:451 according to its own manner by an obscure distinction of the power of judgment, which it calls feeling: that all representations that come to us without our choosing[r] (like those of the senses) enable us to cognize objects only as they affect us, while what they may be in themselves remains unknown to us; and hence that, as far as representations of this kind are concerned, even with the most strenuous attentiveness and distinctness that the understanding may ever add, we can achieve only cognition of *appearances*, never of *things in themselves*. Once this difference has been noticed (maybe merely because of the dissimilarity noted between representations that are given to us from elsewhere, and in which we are passive, from those that we produce solely from ourselves, and in which we prove our activity), it follows of itself that one must concede and assume behind the appearances something else that is not appearance, namely the things in themselves; even if – since they can never become known to us, but only ever how they affect us – we of ourselves rest content with being unable to get any closer to them or ever to know what they are in themselves. This must yield a distinction, however rough, of a *world of sense* from the *world of understanding*, the first of which can be very dissimilar according to the dissimilar sensibility of many kinds of observers of the world, whereas the second, which is its foundation, always remains the same. A human being cannot even – according to the acquaintance he has with himself by inner sensation – presume to cognize how he himself is in himself. For since he does not as it were create himself, and gets his concept not a priori but empirically, it

---

[r] *ohne unsere Willkür*

is natural that about himself too he can gather intelligence only through the inner sense, and consequently only through the appearance of his nature, and the way in which his consciousness is affected; whereas beyond these characteristics of his own subject that are composed of nothing but sundry appearances he must necessarily assume something else lying at its foundation, namely his I, such as it may be in itself; and with respect to mere perception and receptivity to sensations he must thus count himself as belonging to the *world of sense*, but with regard to what there may be of pure activity in him (what reaches consciousness not by affection of the senses, but immediately) as belonging to the *intellectual world*, with which he is yet no further acquainted.

A thinking human being must draw this kind of inference about all the things that occur to him; presumably it is also to be found in the 4:452 commonest understanding, which is known to be much inclined to expect behind the objects of the senses something invisible, and active by itself, but spoils it again by soon making this invisible thing sensuous again, i.e. by wanting to make it an object of intuition, and thus does not thereby become by any degree wiser.

Now, a human being actually does find in himself a capacity by which he is distinguished from all other things, even from himself, in so far as he is affected by objects, and that is *reason*. As pure self-activity, it is elevated even above the *understanding* in this: that though the latter is also self-activity and does not, like sense, contain merely representations that arise when one is affected by things (and thus passive), still it can produce from its activity no other concepts than those which serve merely *to bring sensuous representations under rules* and thereby to unite them in one consciousness, and without this use of sensibility it would think nothing at all; whereas reason under the name of the ideas shows a spontaneity so pure that thereby he[s] goes far beyond anything that sensibility can ever afford him, and provides proof of its foremost occupation by distinguishing the world of sense and the world of understanding from each other, and thereby marking out limits for the understanding itself.

On account of this a rational being must view itself, *as an intelligence* (thus not from the side of its lower powers), as belonging not to the world of sense, but to that of understanding; and hence it has two standpoints from

---

[s] i.e. a human being goes beyond anything that sensibility can ever afford him. Alternatively, the pronouns might refer to the use (*der Gebrauch*) of reason. Many editors feel compelled to change the text to make it refer to reason (*die Vernunft*) in both cases: "that thereby it ... it"

which it can consider itself, and recognize laws for the use of its powers, and consequently for all its actions: *first*, in so far as it belongs to the world of sense, under laws of nature (heteronomy), *secondly*, as belonging to the intelligible world, under laws that, independent of nature, are not empirical, but have their foundation merely in reason.

As a rational being, hence as one that belongs to the intelligible world, a human being can never think of the causality of his own will otherwise than under the idea of freedom; for independence from the determining causes of the world of sense (such as reason must always ascribe to itself) is freedom. Now, with the idea of freedom the concept of *autonomy* is inseparably bound up, and with it the universal principle of morality, 4:453 which in the idea lies at the foundation of all actions of *rational* beings, just as the law of nature lies at the foundation of all appearances.

The suspicion we stirred above has now been removed, as though our inference from freedom to autonomy and from it to the moral law contained a covert circle, namely that perhaps we were presupposing the idea of freedom only for the sake of the moral law, in order afterwards in turn to infer it from freedom, and hence were unable to state any ground of it, but could assume it only as the petitio of a principle^t that well-disposed souls might gladly concede, but which we could never establish as a demonstrable proposition. For now we see that, when we think of ourselves as free, we transfer ourselves as members into the world of understanding, and cognize autonomy of the will, along with its consequence, morality; but if we think of ourselves as bound by duty we consider ourselves as belonging to the world of sense and yet at the same time to the world of understanding.

How is a categorical imperative possible?

A rational being counts itself as an intelligence among the world of understanding and, merely as an efficient cause that belongs to it, it calls its causality a *will*. Yet from the other side it is also conscious of itself as a piece of the world of sense, in which its actions are found as mere appearances of that causality, but their possibility from it, with which we are not acquainted, cannot be understood; rather, those actions as belonging to the world of sense must instead be understood as determined by other

---

^t *Erbittung eines Princips*, i.e. one would be begging the question in assuming this principle. Note also that the German sentence is somewhat incomplete. Inserting "assume" (*annehmen*) resolves the matter.

appearances, namely desires and inclinations. As a mere member of the world of understanding all my actions would therefore conform perfectly with the principle of autonomy of the pure will; as a mere piece of the world of sense they would have to be taken to conform entirely with the natural law of desires and inclinations, and hence with the heteronomy of nature. (The first would rest on the supreme principle of morality, the second on that of happiness.) But since *the world of understanding contains the ground of the world of sense, and hence also of its laws,* and thus is immediately legislating with regard to my will (which belongs wholly to the world of understanding), and thus must also be thought of as such, I shall cognize myself as an intelligence, though on the other side as a being belonging to the world of sense, as still subject to the law of the former – i.e. the world of 4:454 reason, which contains its law in the idea of freedom – and thus to the autonomy of the will; and must consequently view the laws of the world of understanding as imperatives for me, and actions that conform with this principle as duties.

And thus categorical imperatives are possible, because the idea of freedom makes me a member of an intelligible world, in virtue of which, if I were that alone, all my actions *would* always conform with the autonomy of the will, but as at the same time I intuit myself as a member of the world of sense, they *ought* to conform with it; and this *categorical* ought represents a synthetic proposition a priori, because to my will affected by sensuous desires there is added the idea of the same will, but belonging to the world of the understanding, pure and practical by itself, which contains the supreme condition of the former according to reason; roughly in the way that concepts of the understanding, which by themselves signify nothing but form of law as such, are added to the intuitions of the world of sense, and thereby make possible synthetic propositions a priori, on which all cognition of a nature rests.

The practical use of common human reason confirms the correctness of this deduction. There is no one, not even the most hardened scoundrel, if only he is otherwise in the habit of using reason, who – when one presents him with examples of probity of purpose, of steadfastness in following good maxims, of compassion and of general benevolence (involving in addition great sacrifices of advantages and comfort) – does not wish that he too might be so disposed. But he cannot easily^u bring this

---

ᵘ *wohl.* Kant is not saying that the scoundrel cannot become a decent person, it is just painful, difficult, and very unlikely.

about in himself, just because of his inclinations and impulses; while at the same time he wishes to be free from such inclinations, which he himself finds burdensome. By this he therefore proves that, with a will free from impulses of sensibility, he transfers himself in thought into an order of things quite different from that of his desires in the field of sensibility, since from that wish he can expect no gratification of his desires – and hence no condition that would satisfy any of his actual or otherwise conceivable inclinations (for the very idea that elicits the wish from him would thereby lose its pre-eminence) – but only a greater inner worth of 4:455 his person. But this better person he believes himself to be when he transfers himself to the standpoint of a member of the world of understanding, as the idea of freedom, i.e. independence from[v] *determining* causes of the world of sense, without his choosing necessitates him to do; and where he is conscious of a good will that, by his own admission, for his evil will, as a member of the world of sense, constitutes the law, the repute of which he recognizes as he transgresses it. The moral ought is thus one's own necessary willing as a member of an intelligible world, and he thinks of it as an ought only in so far as he considers himself at the same time as a member of the world of sense.

On the extreme boundary of all practical philosophy

All human beings think of themselves as having a will that is free. From this stem all judgments about actions such that they *ought* to have been *done* even if they *were not done*. Even so, this freedom is no experiential concept, and cannot actually be one, since it always remains,[w] even though experience shows the opposite of those demands that are represented as necessary under this presupposition. On the other side it is equally necessary that everything that happens should without fail be determined according to laws of nature, and this natural necessity is no experiential concept either, precisely because it carries with it the concept of necessity, and hence of an a priori cognition. But this concept of a nature is confirmed by experience and unavoidably must itself be presupposed if experience – i.e. cognition of objects of the senses cohering according to universal laws – is to be possible. That is why freedom is only an *idea* of reason, the objective reality of which is in itself doubtful,

---

[v] second edition; the first simply reads "freedom from"
[w] the concept of freedom or perhaps the free will

whereas nature is *a concept of the understanding* that proves, and must necessarily prove, its reality in examples of experience.

Even though there arises from this a dialectic of reason, as with regard to the will the freedom ascribed to it seems to be in contradiction with natural necessity and, at this intersection, reason for *speculative purposes* finds the route of natural necessity much more even and useful than that of freedom: yet for *practical purposes* the footpath of freedom is the only one on which it is possible to make use of one's reason in our behavior; 4:456 which is why it is just as impossible for the subtlest philosophy as for the commonest human reason to rationalize freedom away. It must therefore presuppose: that no true contradiction can be found between freedom and natural necessity of just the same human actions, for it cannot give up the concept of nature, any more than that of freedom.

However, this seeming contradiction must at least be convincingly eliminated, even if one should never be able to comprehend how freedom is possible. For if even the thought of freedom contradicts itself, or nature, which is equally necessary, it would have to be given up altogether in favor of natural necessity.

But it is impossible to steer clear of this contradiction if the subject who deems himself free were to think of himself *in the same sense*, or *in just the same relation* when he calls himself free, as when he takes himself to be subject to the law of nature with respect to the same action. That is why it is an indispensable task of speculative philosophy: at least to show that its deception concerning the contradiction rests in this, that we think a human being in a different sense and relation when we call him free from when we take him, as a piece of nature, to be subject to its laws, and that both not only *can* very well coexist, but also must be thought *as necessarily united* in the same subject, because otherwise no ground could be stated why we should burden reason with an idea that, even if it can *without contradiction* be united with another that is sufficiently validated, still entangles us in a business that puts reason in its theoretical use in a very tight corner. This duty, however, is incumbent upon speculative philosophy only so that it may clear the way for practical philosophy. Thus it is not left to the philosopher's discretion whether he wants to remove the seeming conflict, or leave it untouched; for in the latter case the theory about this is a bonum vacans,[x] of which the fatalist can with

---

[x] an unclaimed good, a good owned by no one; traditionally opposed to a public good, which is jointly owned by all

good reason seize possession and chase all moral science from its sup-posed property as possessing it without title.

Yet one still cannot say that the boundary of practical philosophy begins at this point. For the settlement of that dispute does not belong to it at all; rather, it just demands of Speculative Reason that she put an end to the 4:457 discord in which she entangles herself in theoretical questions, so that Practical Reason may enjoy rest and security from external attacks that could bring into dispute the ground on which she wants to settle.

But the legitimate claim even of common human reason to freedom of the will is founded on the consciousness and the granted presupposition of the independence of reason from merely subjectively determining causes, which together one and all constitute what merely belongs to sensation, and hence under the general label of sensibility. A human being who considers himself in this way as an intelligence thereby puts himself in a different order of things and in a relation to determining grounds of an entirely different kind, when he thinks of himself as an intelligence endowed with a will, and consequently with causality, than when he perceives himself as a phenomenon in the world of sense (which he actually is as well) and subjects his causality, according to external determination, to laws of nature. Now, he soon becomes aware that both can, and indeed even must, take place at the same time. For that a *thing in the appearance* (belonging to the world of sense) is subject to certain laws from which just the same *as a thing* or a being *in itself* is independent, contains not the least contradiction; however, that he must represent and think of himself in this twofold way rests, as regards the first on consciousness of himself as an object affected through the senses, as regards the second on the consciousness of himself as an intelligence, i.e. as independent of sensuous impressions in the use of reason (hence as belonging to the world of understanding).

That is why a human being presumes for himself a will that lets nothing belonging merely to his desires and inclinations be put on its account, and on the contrary thinks possible – indeed even necessary – through himself actions that can be done only by setting aside all desires and sensuous stimulations. Their causality lies in him as an intelligence and in the laws of effects and actions according to principles of an intelligible world, of which he may well know nothing more than that solely reason, and indeed pure reason independent of sensibility, gives the law in it; and likewise that since there, just as an intelligence, he is the actual self (whereas as a human being he is just appearance of himself), those laws concern him immediately and categorically, so that what inclinations and impulses (hence the whole nature of the world of sense) stimulate him to do cannot infringe the laws of his willing as an intelligence; even to the extent that 4:458 he does not answer for the former or attribute them to his actual self, i.e. to his will, as opposed to the lenience he would show them if he conceded to them influence on his maxims to the disadvantage of the rational laws of his will.

By *thinking* itself into a world of understanding practical reason does not at all overstep its boundaries; but it would if it wanted to *look* or *sense* itself *into it*. The former is only a negative thought, with regard to the world of sense, which gives reason no laws in determining the will, and is positive only in this one point: that freedom, as a negative determination, is at the same time combined with a (positive) capacity and even with a causality of reason, which we call a will, so to act that the principle of actions conforms with the essential characteristic of a rational cause, i.e. with the condition of universal validity of the maxim, as a law. But if it were to fetch in addition an *object of the will*, i.e. a motive, from the world of understanding, then it would overstep its bounds, and presume acquaintance with something of which it knows nothing. The concept of a world of understanding is thus only a *standpoint* that reason sees itself necessitated to take outside appearances, *in order to think of itself as practical*, and this would not be possible if the influences of sensibility were determining for a human being, and yet it is necessary in so far as he is not to be denied consciousness of himself, as an intelligence, and hence as a rational cause active through reason, i.e. operating freely. Of course, this thought leads to the idea of another order and legislation than that of the mechanism of nature, which applies to the world of sense, and makes necessary the concept of an intelligible world (i.e. the whole of rational beings, as things in themselves), but without the least presumption to think of it further than merely according to its *formal* condition, i.e. to the universality of the maxim of the will, as a law, and hence to the autonomy of the latter, which alone is consistent with its freedom; whereas all laws that are determined with reference to an object yield heteronomy, which can be found only in laws of nature and also apply only to the world of sense.

But reason would overstep all its bounds if it undertook to *explain* **how** pure reason can be practical, which would be one and the same task 4:459 entirely as to explain *how freedom is possible*.

For we can explain nothing but what we can trace back to laws whose object can be given in some possible experience. But freedom is a mere idea, the objective reality of which can in no way be established according to laws of nature, and hence not in any possible experience either; which can thus never be comprehended or even just inspected because it can never be underpinned by an example of anything analogous. It holds only as a necessary presupposition of reason in a being that believes itself to be conscious of a will, i.e. of a capacity distinct from a mere desiderative faculty (namely to determine itself to action as an intelligence, hence according to laws of reason, independently of natural instincts). But where determination by laws of nature ceases, there all *explanation* ceases as well, and nothing is left but *defense*, i.e. warding off the objections of those who pretend to have looked deeper into the essence of things, and therefore boldly declare freedom to be impossible. One can only show them that the contradiction they have supposedly discovered in it lies nowhere else than in this, that in order to make the law of nature hold with regard to human actions, they necessarily had to consider the human being as an appearance; and that now, as one demands that as an intelligence they think of him also as a thing in itself, they continue to consider him as an appearance all the same, in which case the separation of his causality (i.e. of his will) from all natural laws of the world of sense in one and the same subject would of course prompt a contradiction; but it vanishes if they were willing to come to their senses and, as is reasonable, admit that behind the appearances there must lie at their foundation the things in themselves (though hidden), and that one cannot demand of their laws of operation^y that they be one and the same as those under which their appearances stand.

The subjective impossibility of *explaining* freedom of the will is the same as the impossibility of detecting and making comprehensible an *interest**

---

* An interest is that by which reason becomes practical, i.e. a cause that determines the will. That is why it is said only of a rational being that it takes an interest in something; non-rational creatures feel only sensuous impulses. Reason takes an immediate interest in the action only when the universal validity of its maxim is a sufficient determining ground of the will. Such an interest alone is pure. But if it can determine the will only by means of another object of desire, or on the presupposition of a special feeling of the subject, then reason takes only a mediate interest in the action; and since reason all by itself, without experience, can detect neither objects of the will nor a special feeling lying at its foundation, this latter interest would only be empirical and not a pure rational interest. The logical interest of reason (to advance its insights) is never immediate, but presupposes purposes of its use.

^y *von deren Wirkungsgesetzen*, the laws that determine their effects

4:460

that a human being could take in moral laws; and even so, he actually does 4:460
take an interest in them, the foundation of which in us we call moral feeling,
which some have falsely proclaimed the standard of our moral judging,
whereas it must rather be viewed as the *subjective* effect that the law
exercises on the will, for which reason alone supplies the objective grounds.

In order to will that for which reason alone prescribes the ought to a
sensuously affected rational being, a capacity of reason to *induce a feeling of
pleasure* or of delight in fulfilling duty it is admittedly needed, and hence a
causality of reason to determine sensibility in conformity with its principles. But it is quite impossible to understand, i.e. to make comprehensible
a priori, how a mere thought, which itself contains nothing sensuous, may
produce a sensation of pleasure or displeasure; for that is a special kind of
causality about which, as about any causality, we can determine nothing
whatsoever a priori, and must therefore consult experience alone. But
since it cannot furnish any relation of cause to effect except between two
objects of experience, whereas here pure reason, by mere ideas (which
for experience yield no object at all), is to be the cause of an effect that
admittedly lies in experience, it is quite impossible for us human beings
to explain how and why the *universality of a maxim as a law*, and hence
morality, interests us. Just this much is certain: it is not *because the law
interests* us that it has validity for us (for that is heteronomy and dependence of practical reason on sensibility, namely on a feeling lying at its 4:461
foundation, in which it could never be morally legislating), but the law
interests because it is valid for us as human beings, since it arose from our
will as an intelligence, hence from our actual self; *but what belongs to mere
appearance is necessarily subordinated by reason to the constitution of the thing
in itself.*

Thus the question: how a categorical imperative is possible, can indeed
be answered to the extent that one can state the one presupposition on
which alone it is possible, namely the idea of freedom, and likewise that
one can also see the necessity of this presupposition, which is sufficient
for the *practical use* of reason, i.e. for the conviction of the *validity of this
imperative*, and hence of the moral law as well; but how this presupposition itself is possible can never be understood by any human reason. But
on the presupposition of the freedom of the will of an intelligence, its
autonomy – as the formal condition under which alone it can be determined – is a necessary consequence. To presuppose this freedom of the
will, moreover, is not only (without falling into contradiction with the

principle of natural necessity in the connection of appearances in the world of sense) quite easily *possible* (as speculative philosophy can show), in the case of a rational being conscious of its causality through reason, and hence of a will (which is distinct from desires) it is also without any further condition *necessary*, to suppose it practically, i.e. in the idea in all the actions he chooses, as their condition. But any human reason is entirely unable to explain *how* pure reason, without other incentives that might be taken from somewhere else, can by itself be practical, i.e. how the mere *principle of the universal validity of all its maxims as laws* (which of course would be the form of a pure practical reason) without any matter (object) of the will, in which one could take some interest in advance, can by itself yield an incentive, and produce an interest that would be called purely *moral*, or in other words: *how pure reason can be practical*; and all the effort and labor of seeking an explanation for it are lost.

4:462   It is just the same as if I sought to fathom how freedom itself as the causality of a will is possible. For then I leave the explanatory ground of philosophy, and have no other. I might indeed flutter about in the intelligible world, in the world of intelligences, which still remains for me; but even though I have an *idea* of it, which is well founded, yet I have not the least *acquaintance* with it, nor can I ever achieve this by all the strivings of my natural rational faculty. It signifies only a something that remains when I have excluded from the determining grounds of my will everything that belongs to the world of sense, merely so as to limit the principle of motives from the field of sensibility by setting its bounds, and by showing that it does not include all in all within itself, but that there is more beyond it still; but with this something more I am no further acquainted. After separating off all matter, i.e. cognition of objects, nothing remains for me of pure reason – which thinks this ideal – but its form, namely the practical law of the universal validity of maxims, and to think of reason, conforming with this, with reference to a pure world of understanding as a possible efficient cause, i.e. one determining the will; here the incentive must be lacking entirely; unless this idea of an intelligible world were itself the incentive, or that in which reason originally takes an interest; but to make this comprehensible is just the problem we cannot solve.

    Here, then, is the supreme boundary of all moral inquiry; and determining it is of great importance just for this purpose alone, that Reason may not, on the one hand, in a manner harmful to morals, search around in the world of sense for the supreme motive and a comprehensible but empirical interest nor, on the other hand, impotently flap her wings without moving from the spot in the space – empty for her – of transcendent concepts, under the name of the intelligible world, and so lose herself among phantasms.[21] Further, the idea of a pure world of understanding as a whole of all intelligences, to which we ourselves belong as rational beings (though on the other side we are also members of the world of sense), remains always a useful and permissible idea for the sake of a rational faith, even if all knowledge ends at its boundary; so as to effect in us a lively interest in the moral law by means of the glorious ideal of a universal kingdom of *ends in themselves* (of rational beings) to which we can belong as members only if we carefully con- 4:463 duct ourselves according to maxims of freedom as if they were laws of nature.

Concluding remark

The speculative use of reason, *with regard to nature*, leads to the absolute necessity of some supreme cause *of the world*; the practical use of reason, *with respect to freedom*, also leads to an absolute necessity, but only *of laws of actions* of a rational being, as such. Now, it is an essential *principle* of all use of our reason to pursue its cognition up to being conscious of its *necessity* (for without it it would not be cognition of reason). But it is an equally essential *limitation* of precisely the same reason that it can see neither the *necessity* of what exists, or what happens, nor of what ought to happen, unless a *condition* under which it exists, or happens, or ought to happen, is available as its foundation. In this way, however, by constant inquiry after the condition, the satisfaction of reason is just postponed further and further. That is why it restlessly seeks the unconditionally necessary and sees itself necessitated to assume it without any means of making it comprehensible to itself; fortunate enough if only it can detect the concept that is compatible with this presupposition. It is therefore no criticism of our deduction of the supreme principle of morality, but an accusation that would have to be brought against human reason as such, that it cannot make comprehensible – as regards its absolute necessity – an unconditional practical law (such as the categorical imperative must be); for that it does not want to do this by a condition, namely by means of some interest at its foundation, cannot be held against it, because it would then not be a moral law, i.e. the supreme law of freedom. And thus we do not indeed comprehend the practical unconditional necessity of the moral imperative, yet we do comprehend its *incomprehensibility*, and this is all that can reasonably be required of a philosophy that in its principles strives up to the boundary of human reason.

Notes

Preface

1. The ancient division of philosophy into physics, ethics, and logic is commonly attributed to Xenocrates (396–314 BC), the third head of Plato's Academy. It was widely accepted in later antiquity, particularly by the Stoics.
2. Kant is referring to the division of labor, which in the late eighteenth century, in the wake of the work of the Scottish philosopher and economist Adam Smith (1723–90), was beginning to affect many areas of human activity.
3. Christian Wolff (1679–1754), the most influential follower of Gottfried Wilhelm Leibniz in Germany, published his *Philosophia Practica Universalis* in 1738–39.
4. Kant finally published two volumes entitled *The Metaphysics of Morals* in 1797. The two books concern legal philosophy (the "Doctrine of Right") and ethics (the "Doctrine of Virtue") respectively. The relationship between the *Groundwork* and the late *Metaphysics of Morals* is not as straightforward as the title of the earlier book may seem to indicate. Note that here and elsewhere, the typographical conventions of the time sometimes make it difficult to decide whether Kant is referring to subject matter or book titles; though the two are, of course, closely connected.
5. It is unclear whether, in 1785, Kant intended to write a separate "Critique of Pure Practical Reason," or whether the *Groundwork* was originally meant to be the sole foundational work in moral philosophy. However, in his 1788 *Critique of Practical* [sic!] *Reason*, he explicitly rejects the very project of a Critique of *pure* practical reason (5:3), and less explicitly the justificatory project of the third section of the *Groundwork* (5:47).
6. The *Critique of Pure Reason*, published in 1781 (second, revised edition 1787). The publication of a critical work in moral philosophy – the

Groundwork – explains why, in retrospect, Kant restricts the scope of the
first *Critique* to "speculative" or theoretical reason.

First section

7. Cf. Matthew 5:43–44, referring back to Leviticus 19:18, and Luke 6:27 and
   6:35.
8. Kant does not explicitly formulate a "first proposition." As a result, it is a
   matter of much scholarly debate which of the principles put forward so far is
   intended for this role.
9. In Plato's *Meno*, Socrates (*ca.* 470–399 BC) teaches an ignorant slave boy to
   double the area of a square by helping him to develop his own mathematical
   potential. This is meant to demonstrate the a priori character of geometry, and
   the pre-existence of the human soul. However, Kant may also be thinking of
   Socrates's professed method of midwifery in the *Theaetetus*. On the "Socratic
   method," see also *Metaphysics of Morals*, 6:411 and 6:479.

Second section

10. Cf. Luke 18:19, Matthew 19:17, and Mark 10:18.
11. Kant is probably referring to an extant letter by the Swiss aesthetician
    Johann Georg Sulzer (1720–79), who was best known for his *Allgemeine
    Theorie der schönen Künste*, published in several installments between 1771
    and 1774. Sulzer's letter bears the date of December 8, 1770. Kant com-
    pleted the manuscript of the *Groundwork* in 1784.
12. The expression "pragmatic history" was coined by the Greek historian
    Polybius (*ca.* 200–118 BC). Its original meaning is a matter of dispute.
    Kant published an *Anthropology from a Pragmatic Point of View* in 1798.
13. The investigation of the possibility of synthetic principles a priori was the
    central task of the *Critique of Pure Reason* (1781/87) and the *Prolegomena*
    (1783).
14. The topic is indeed taken up again in the late *Metaphysics of Morals*, 6:240
    and 6:390–391.
15. *Selbsthalterin* was an epithet of the Russian empress. Kant may have asso-
    ciated the term with Catherine the Great (1729–96).
16. In Pindar's second Pythian Ode, a vengeful Jupiter deceives the mythical
    Greek king Ixion into making love to a cloud, which he takes to be Jupiter's
    wife, the goddess Juno.
17. A position Kant associates with ancient ethics, particularly the hedonism of
    Epicurus (341–270 BC).
18. In *An Inquiry into the Original of Our Ideas of Beauty and Virtue* (1725) and
    *An Essay on the Nature and Conduct of the Passions and Affections, with
    Illustrations on the Moral Sense* (1728), the Scottish philosopher Francis

Hutcheson (1694–1747) maintained that moral judgment and moral motivation are not brought about by reason, but by a moral sense which effects
that benevolence pleases us.

19. Kant has Christian Wolff and the Stoics in mind, cf. the table of erroneous
ethical theories in the *Critique of Practical Reason* 5:40.

20. The table in the *Critique of Practical Reason* reveals Kant's target to be the
German philosopher Christian August Crusius (1715–75).

Third section

21. In the *Critique of Pure Reason*, Kant warns us not to leave the world of
experience behind, like Plato on the "wings of the forms" (or "ideas"), who
was hoping to make better metaphysical progress in the pure world of the
understanding (cf. A5/B9).

Selected glossary

access	Eingang
acquaintance	Kenntnis
act (n.)	Actus
action	Handlung
activity	Tätigkeit
actuality	Wirklichkeit
advance (vb.)	befördern
advancement	Beförderung
agreeable	angenehm
appearance	Erscheinung
author	Urheber, Verfasser
beneficence	Wohltat, Wohltun
benevolence	Wohlwollen
bind (vb.)	verbinden
bound(ary)	Grenze
capability	Fähigkeit
capacity	Vermögen, cf. faculty
cause (n.)	Ursache
choice	Willkür, Wahl
choose	wählen
cognition	Erkenntnis
cognize	erkennen
compassion	Teilnehmung
conclusion	Folgerung, Ausgang
condition	Bedingung, Zustand

conformity with law	Gesetzmäßigkeit
connection	Verknüpfung
consequence	Folge
constraint	Zwang
corroboration	Festsetzung
counsel	Anratung, Ratschlag
desiderative faculty	Begehrungsvermögen
desire	Begierde
determination	Bestimmung, cf. function
determine	bestimmen
determining ground	Bestimmungsgrund
dignity	Würde
displeasure	Unlust
disposition	Gesinnung
disrespect	Nichtachtung
division	Abteilung, Einteilung
doctrine	Lehre
duty	Pflicht
effect (n.)	Wirkung
end (n.)	Zweck, Ende
endowment	Ausstattung
enjoyment	Genuß
evil (n.)	Böses
example	Beispiel
experience	Erfahrung
experiential concept	Erfahrungsbegriff
explanation, explication	Erklärung
faculty	Vermögen, cf. capacity
faith	Glaube
feasibility	Tunlichkeit
feeling	Gefühl
fitness	Tauglichkeit
fittingness	Schicklichkeit
function	Bestimmung, cf. determination
general	allgemein, cf. universal
good fortune	Glück
gratification	Vergnügen

guidance	Lenkung, Leitung
guideline	Leitfaden
happiness	Glückseligkeit
honest	ehrlich
human	menschlich
human being	Mensch
humanity	Menschheit, Menschen
identification	Aufsuchung
ill (n.)	Übel
impulse	Antrieb
incentive	Triebfeder
inclination	Neigung
innocence	Unschuld
insight	Einsicht
intention	Absicht, Vorsatz, cf. purpose
intuition	Anschauung
joy	Freude
judging (n.)	Beurteilung
judgment	Urteil
kingdom	Reich
know	wissen
knowledge	Wissen
legislation	Gesetzgebung
legislator	Gesetzgeber
legitimate claim	Rechtsanspruch
limit (n.)	Schranke
limitation	Einschränkung
measure	Maß, Maßstab
mind	Geist, Gemüt
moral science	Moral
morality	Sittlichkeit, Moralität
morals	Sitten
motivating ground	Bewegungsgrund
necessitation	Nötigung
necessity	Notwendigkeit
need	Bedürfnis
object	Gegenstand, Objekt

obligation	Verbindlichkeit
omission	Unterlassung
perception	Wahrnehmung
perfect	vollkommen
perfection	Vollkommenheit
philosophy	Philosophie, Weltweisheit
please	gefallen
pleasure	Lust
power	Kraft, Macht
prescription	Vorschrift
presupposition	Voraussetzung
principle	Grundsatz, Prinzip
propensity	Hang
proposition	Satz
prudence	Klugheit
purity	Reinigkeit, Lauterkeit
purpose	Absicht, cf. intention
purposive	zweckmäßig
reality	Realität
reason (n.)	Vernunft
reasonable	billig
receptivity	Empfänglichkeit
representation	Vorstellung
respect (n.)	Achtung
right (n.)	Recht
righteousness	Rechtschaffenheit
sanctity	Heiligkeit
satisfaction	Befriedigung
self-activity	Selbsttätigkeit
self-conceit	Eigendünkel
self-love	Selbstliebe
sensation	Empfindung
sense(s)	Sinn(e)
sensibility	Sinnlichkeit
separation	Absonderung
spontaneity	Spontaneität
standard	Richtmaß

stimulation	Anreiz, Anreizung, Reiz
sublimity	Erhabenheit
supreme	oberst
sympathy	Sympathie
transition	Übergang
understanding	Verstand
union	Verbindung
universal	allgemein (cf. general)
universal validity	Allgemeingültigkeit, allgemeine Gültigkeit
use (n.)	Gebrauch
validity	Gültigkeit
vice	Laster
virtue	Tugend
will (n.)	Wille
willing (n.)	Wollen
worth (n.)	Wert
worthiness	Würdigkeit

Index

Cambridge Texts in the History of Philosophy

Titles published in the series thus far